MICHAEL MICHAELY
THE HEBREW UNIVERSITY OF JERUSALEM

BALANCE-OF-PAYMENTS ADJUSTMENT POLICIES:

Japan, Germany, and the Netherlands

OCCASIONAL PAPER 106

NATIONAL BUREAU OF ECONOMIC RESEARCH
NEW YORK 1968
Distributed by COLUMBIA UNIVERSITY PRESS
NEW YORK AND LONDON

RELATION OF THE DIRECTORS TO THE WORK AND PUBLICATIONS OF THE NATIONAL BUREAU OF ECONOMIC RESEARCH

1. The object of the National Bureau of Economic Research is to ascertain and to present to the public important economic facts and their interpretation in a scientific and impartial manner. The Board of Directors is charged with the responsibility of ensuring that the work of the National Bureau is carried on in strict conformity with this object.
2. To this end the Board of Directors shall appoint one or more Directors of Research.
3. The Director or Directors of Research shall submit to the members of the Board, or to its Executive Committee, for their formal adoption, all specific proposals concerning researches to be instituted.
4. No report shall be published until the Director or Directors of Research shall have submitted to the Board a summary drawing attention to the character of the data and their utilization in the report, the nature and treatment of the problems involved, the main conclusions, and such other information as in their opinion would serve to determine the suitability of the report for publication in accordance with the principles of the National Bureau.
5. A copy of any manuscript proposed for publication shall also be submitted to each member of the Board. For each manuscript to be so submitted a special committee shall be appointed by the President, or at his designation by the Executive Director, consisting of three Directors selected as nearly as may be one from each general division of the Board. The names of the special manuscript committee shall be stated to each Director when the summary and report described in paragraph (4) are sent to him. It shall be the duty of each member of the committee to read the manuscript. If each member of the special committee signifies his approval within thirty days, the manuscript may be published. If each member of the special committee has not signified his approval within thirty days of the transmittal of the report and manuscript, the Director of Research shall then notify each member of the Board, requesting approval or disapproval of publication, and thirty additional days shall be granted for this purpose. The manuscript shall then not be published unless at least a majority of the entire Board and a two-thirds majority of those members of the Board who shall have voted on the proposal within the time fixed for the receipt of votes on the publication proposed shall have approved.
6. No manuscript may be published, though approved by each member of the special committee, until forty-five days have elapsed from the transmittal of the summary and report. The interval is allowed for the receipt of any memorandum of dissent or reservation, together with a brief statement of his reasons, that any member may wish to express; and such memorandum of dissent or reservation shall be published with the manuscript if he so desires. Publication does not, however, imply that each member of the Board has read the manuscript, or that either members of the Board in general, or of the special committee, have passed upon its validity in every detail.
7. A copy of this resolution shall, unless otherwise determined by the Board, be printed in each copy of every National Bureau book.

(Resolution adopted October 25, 1926, as revised February 6, 1933, and February 24, 1941)

CONTENTS

TABLES

CHARTS

ACKNOWLEDGMENTS

Among the debts I have accumulated in the course of this study, the heaviest is owed to Hal B. Lary. He was instrumental in getting the project started and was a source of continuous encouragement. His aid, ranging from advice on fundamental issues to minute details, was indeed invaluable.

I have been fortunate in being able to consult a most distinguished panel of economists, who volunteered to serve on the study's Advisory Committee: Peter B. Kenen (chairman), Arthur I. Bloomfield, J. Marcus Fleming, George Garvy, Gottfried Haberler, Charles P. Kindleberger, Irving B. Kravis, Fritz Machlup, and Robert Triffin. Their discussions, both in and outside committee meetings, have helped substantially in clarifying the framework of the study, indicating avenues of investigation, checking the findings, and improving the quality of their presentation. The present monograph has also benefited materially from the penetrating comments and constructive suggestions of the National Bureau staff reading committee, which consisted of Irving B. Kravis, Robert E. Lipsey, and Ilse Mintz. Many other colleagues at the National Bureau, in particular Phillip Cagan, have also offered valuable advice. I also wish to thank Lester V. Chandler, Walter W. Heller, and Joseph H. Willits, who comprised the reading committee of the National Bureau's Board of Directors.

I have had the opportunity to offer oral presentations of the study at various stages, and have learned much in the process. Besides staff meetings at the National Bureau, such discussions took place in seminars at the University of Chicago, Columbia University, Harvard University, M.I.T., Princeton University, Rutgers University, and the World Bank.

It is a pleasure to acknowledge my indebtedness to Maxine Nord, my research assistant in this project, for carrying out effectively and patiently the tedious task of compiling and manipulating the mass of data involved in the study; to Gerald Paul for editing the manuscript; and to H. Irving Forman for skillfully drawing the charts.

Finally, I wish to thank the Hebrew University of Jerusalem, which granted me an extended leave, and the Ford Foundation, which undertook the support of this study as part of the National Bureau's program of international economic studies. Without this combination of the essential ingredients of time and financial resources, a study of even much smaller dimensions would not have been feasible.

MICHAEL MICHAELY

1

INTRODUCTION AND SUMMARY

Policies for the appropriate adjustment of imbalances of payments, in connection with policies for international liquidity, have been widely discussed since the end of World War I. Prior to that time it had been assumed that the gold standard provided the necessary adjustment mechanism automatically. In recent years the issue has acquired a particular urgency and has attracted a great deal of attention. However, in contrast to the intensive investigation of the liquidity issue, there have actually been very few studies of the state of adjustment policies. In view of the importance of this area for the conduct of international economic relations by the United States as well as other countries, the National Bureau has chosen adjustment policies as one of the topics for analysis in its program of international economic studies.[1]

This report investigates the recent pattern of balance-of-payments adjustment policies. Determining the pattern of policies in actual use is an essential part of evaluating the policies, arrangements, and institutions needed to improve the international monetary mechanism and assure an optimal flow of international transactions. In particular, the experience of other countries may help to indicate the potential of various policies which the United States might employ, in its effort to reconcile maximum utilization of economic capacity and a rapid rate of growth with the compelling need for balance-of-payments adjustment.

The over-all plan of the study, of which this is a preliminary report, is twofold. First, each individual country will be analyzed separately in order to identify the policy reactions in the country. Following this, a synthesis of the individual studies will be attempted, in order

[1] See Hal B. Lary, *Problems of the United States as World Trader and Banker*, New York, National Bureau of Economic Research, 1963; particularly pp. 113–117.

to search for any general pattern, or patterns, in the international monetary system as a whole and to analyze the reasons for similarities or differences among countries.

This latter part, or over-all study, will take up such questions as whether the policies undertaken to adjust deficits and surpluses in the balance of payments are symmetrical to each other, or whether deficits and surpluses provoke different kinds of reactions; whether or not countries employ any strategy or strategies which assign certain policy instruments to balance-of-payments adjustment while reserving others for domestic targets; whether any general change in the policy pattern was discernible over the period under consideration; and if variables such as the size of trade or recent experiences with inflations and depressions explain differences in policy patterns among countries. Other questions of a similar nature will also be investigated.

It must be emphasized that the study of individual countries is subordinated to the ultimate purpose of an over-all analysis of the international monetary system. The separate studies will thus follow a uniform method, making it possible to incorporate them into a wider analysis later. In the process, much specific information about each country will inevitably be lost. In particular, each individual study does not purport to be a comprehensive description and analysis of all the policy actions taken by the country in question to adjust balance-of-payments disturbances. Such a comprehensive study of any single country would require much more attention than could be given to individual cases in an analysis of the present nature. In the present study, the individual patterns are, rather, presented with the aim of demarcating the most salient features of the system. This approach involved selecting certain policies for observation and excluding others: it led to a concentration on aggregative monetary and fiscal measures, with only scant attention to other policies. The study may thus be described as being, essentially, the identification and analysis of the pattern of use of financial policies for balance-of-payments adjustment.

It is, basically, a statistical undertaking. The analysis is aimed at discovering causal connections in one direction: from imbalances of payments to policy measures. It starts out with the assumption that, over time, a consistent association in the occurrence of a certain development, or position, of the balance of payments (or of any other economic target), with the movements of a policy variable indicates a causal relationship rather than a coincidence. The study of time series of variables which indicate balance-of-payments disturbances and those which represent policy instruments may thus reveal the policy re-actions—be they automatic policy responses or ad hoc decisions—to im-balances of payments. The investigation of possible associations is conducted by a number of methods; all of these are rather crude, pri-marily owing to the small number of observations in each country and the large coverage of the study. Yet in combination they appear to yield meaningful results.

The present paper is an interim report on the over-all study. It dis-cusses, in Chapter 2, the methods and techniques of analysis, the meaning of balance-of-payments "disturbances" and their identifica-tion, the nature of the policy variables used for adjustment and the interpretation of an adjustment policy, and the possible limitations of the study, its major deficiencies, and the qualifications which must be attached to its conclusions. Chapters 3, 4, and 5 present, as a sam-ple, the analyses of three countries: Japan, Germany, and the Nether-lands. At this stage of reporting, no similar sample could be offered of the analysis which will follow in the final report. International com-parisons and implications for the international monetary system as a whole must await the completion of all the intended individual country studies.

Of the three countries presented here, one—Germany—does not ap-pear to have conducted any systematic policy of balance-of-payments adjustment. During about half of the period covered—throughout most of the 1950's—Germany had a practically uninterrupted surplus in its balance of payments. Yet economic policy does not seem to have re-sponded by taking an expansive direction—a response that would have been required to restore balance-of-payments equilibrium. The con-tinuous and substantial accumulation of foreign-exchange reserves was apparently regarded as a favorable development rather than as a disturbance which should be corrected. In other periods too, fluc-tuations in the balance-of-payments position do not appear to have triggered adjustments of policy measures with any consistency. In Ger-many financial policy thus seems to have been unresponsive, by and large, to balance-of-payments developments.

In Japan and the Netherlands an entirely different pattern is revealed. Here, monetary policy appears to be geared quite closely to fluctuations in the balance of payments. The working of the monetary mechanism is not entirely similar in the two countries, but they share two major elements: the discount rate and money supply react in a consistent way to balance-of-payments disturbances. In times of a deficit, the discount rate is raised and the rate of expansion of money supply tends to fall; with balance-of-payments surpluses, the tendencies are reversed. These are responses which work in the direction of balance-of-payments adjustment. Although changes in the discount rate are of course decided upon directly by the respective central banks, the changes in money supply take place automatically as a result of movements of foreign-exchange reserves. Commercial banks partly offset the automatic impact on the credit basis by increasing their borrowing from the central bank when foreign-exchange reserves fall and repaying their debts when reserves rise. In the Netherlands, this offsetting is even helped by a policy of lowering the minimum-reserve ratio of commercial banks when the balance of payments is in deficit, and raising the ratio at times of surpluses. Both in Japan and in the Netherlands, commercial bank credit thus fulfills only a minor role in the adjustment process, and central bank credit even tends, almost invariably, to move contrary to the direction of movement of foreign-exchange reserves. By some definitions, this may be termed a "disadjusting," or "neutralizing," monetary policy, yet the discount rate and money supply do tend to move in an adjusting direction. By the definition suggested in this study, this outcome amounts to an adherence to the classical "rules of the game."

In neither Japan nor the Netherlands does fiscal policy appear to be attuned to balance-of-payments adjustment. In all three countries, fiscal policy is apparently considered a tool which cannot, or should not, respond to balance-of-payments fluctuations. Nor does fiscal policy appear to form generally part of a policy "mix," by which domestic targets are assigned to fiscal policy whereas monetary policy is reserved for balance-of-payments adjustments, although a few episodes in Japan and the Netherlands do tend to follow this pattern. In the main, the principle of a balanced budget was followed in all three countries, and budgetary policy does not appear to have been generally used for short-term targets.

2

APPROACH, CONCEPTS, AND
METHODS

1. Coverage of the Study: Countries and Period

The criteria used for selection of countries for observation are dictated by the purposes of the over-all study. They must be large countries in terms of size of international transactions: if implications for the international monetary system as a whole are to be drawn, it is obviously more practical to concentrate on countries whose impact on this system is large. Preferably, the countries should also resemble the United States in structure and circumstances. For these reasons, the study is planned to cover the major trading, industrial countries commonly known as the "Group of Ten." (For reasons which will be explained later, however, one member of the group—Canada—will be excluded.)

The countries which will eventually be covered conduct, in their aggregate, an overwhelming share of world trade and other international transactions, own an overwhelming share of the world's capital, hold most of the world's international liquidity, and produce most of the world's income. Conclusions which are valid for these countries as an aggregate are thus applicable, by and large, to the international monetary system as a whole.

The period selected is that following World War II. The experience of earlier periods is not entirely irrelevant, but of less immediate application to current issues and to problems which are likely to be faced in the near future.[1] The earlier postwar years of 1945–49 were

---

[1] The experience of earlier periods has been investigated in two well-known studies whose methods are similar in essence to the one adopted here, although confined primarily to observations of a single policy variable. The interwar period was the topic of Ragnar Nurkse's classic study, *International Currency Experience* (League of Nations, 1944), where this method of investigation was followed in Chapter IV. The prewar period was studied in Arthur I. Bloomfield, *Monetary Policy under the Gold Standard: 1880–1914* (Federal Reserve Bank of New York, 1959), particularly Chapter V. These studies will be referred to later.

excluded too, on similar grounds. Circumstances in those years were definitely unique; although one cannot safely predict that they may not recur, it seems quite evident that such repetition is not likely in the near future, so that any conclusions derived from the experience of those years is bound to be of lesser importance for current economic problems. The study thus starts with the year 1950 and ends with the latest date for which information was available at the time of its collection, which would usually be the end of 1965 or the beginning of 1966.[2]

2. The General Approach

As indicated above, the study will seek to identify the policies followed in various countries at times of imbalances of payments. It will try to find what policy measures were commonly taken in such times, and whether these could be expected to lead to balance-of-payments adjustment. The study will hence attempt to establish probable relationships between the position of the balance of payments and the policies undertaken: it will try to reveal the principles followed by studying the actual behavior. The analysis will be of a statistical nature.

It should be emphasized that the analysis is confined to the search for causal associations in one direction: changes in the target variable are the cause and changes in policy variables are the effect. Although the study does *not* address itself primarily to the effect of policy measures on the target, indirectly the findings may provide at least some indication of the measure of success of the policies followed. Knowing the typical policy patterns of governments, and comparing them with the balance-of-payments experiences of the respective countries, may provide some clues about the effects of policies on the balance of payments. The international comparisons which will follow the studies of individual countries may thus make some contribution toward this end.

When a consistent relationship between the movement of a policy variable and imbalances of payments is established, this finding will be tentatively interpreted as an indication of a causal relationship. That

---

[2] In a few instances, later data have been added to the study without being consistently incorporated into the analysis.

is, if a policy instrument reacts consistently to balance-of-payments disturbances by moving in a certain direction, it will be assumed that this is not a coincidence but that the reaction was causally related to the disturbance, and is, therefore, conscious behavior on the part of policy designers. An attempt will usually be made, in such a case, to give a possible explanation for their conduct; that is, to see what model, or analytical structure, could be expected to yield this pattern of action. The models could, of course, be different for different countries—and in each country, for different periods or different governments. The study will thus not try to "impose" one model upon all situations; nor will it try to assess the theoretical credibility of any model which may be revealed. The purpose will be to establish what policy makers may have wished and anticipated, rather than to evaluate whether their actions were well-founded.

More generally, this study does *not* aim to pass judgment on the actions of governments of the countries under investigation—either on the targets they have been pursuing or on the means selected to achieve them. True, in some final analysis, such a judgment must be made. Studying past experience in order to improve future performance necessarily implies pointing out favorable and beneficial patterns of behavior and setting them off from those which lead away from the desirable goals. The present study, however, is viewed only as a preliminary, necessary step in such an assessment; it is concerned only with the attempt to find out what the policies actually were, rather than with the subsequent question of which of these policies were "good," or "bad"—and why. This definition of the subject matter of the study probably cannot be overemphasized, particularly because the analytical method may lead the unwary reader in the opposite direction. The constant attempt to search for a positive relationship between balance-of-payments disturbances and policy actions may easily create the impression that the existence of such a relationship is regarded favorably, while the lack of it is scorned. It should therefore be repeated that no such normative judgment is intended in the present study.

The study's emphasis throughout will be on the relationship between policy instruments and the balance of payments. In addition, however, a few other major economic targets will be observed. This will serve two functions. One is to make certain that a consistent association between imbalances of payments and a certain policy variable could not be attributed to the impact of another target variable. To cite an obvious example: If the balance-of-payments surplus is positively correlated with the rate of unemployment, measures taken to relieve either unemployment or excess demand for labor, when investigated in isolation, would be erroneously interpreted as being intended for the sake of balance-of-payments equilibrium. The other purpose of observing competing target variables is to find out whether the absence of a consistent relationship between the imbalances of payments and a given policy instrument could be due to the employment of this policy instrument in the service of an alternative policy target.

It should be understood, however, that these are only auxiliary observations, not on a par—in the present study—with the direct investigation of the relationship between policy instruments and balance-of-payments disturbances. In other words, this study is not a general investigation of trade-offs among targets or of the over-all allocation of policy instruments. It is designed specifically to observe reactions to imbalances of payments; other policy targets are admitted only as a means of ascertaining, and possibly explaining, the existence of certain reactions or their absence.

3. The Analytical Method

The basic information on which the analysis will rest consists of quarterly data (adjusted for seasonal variations, where these are found). Quarters have been selected, rather than months, for a number of reasons. Some data, mainly in the fiscal sphere but also on the balance of payments, are usually available quarterly but rarely on a monthly basis. Even when monthly data are available, their use and manipulation would be highly cumbersome. Moreover, an important consideration is the presumption that monthly data may reflect a strong element of chance, erratic variations, whereas the aggregation of data into quarters helps in smoothing out these random fluctuations.

While the quarter is the basic unit for data compilation, the study of interrelationships among variables *within* each quarter could hardly be of great significance. The quarter is an arbitrary dissection of the continuum of time. Changes in policy variables could easily be due to movements of the policy targets in the previous quarter, or even in still earlier periods. If these movements should change direction often from one quarter to another, observations of relationships would be very likely to yield misleading results.

In recent years, a few attempts have been made to construct a "reaction function" for various policy instruments by regression analysis, using forms of distributed lags to take account of the problem just cited.[3] While an approach along these lines is conceivable, the extremely large measure of experimentation which would have been required for each country, among other things, would make this a much too ambitious undertaking for the present study. It would, by its character, also have one major drawback for the study's purposes: it would cram the information about policy reactions into a single measure, without distinctions among chronological periods or between periods of upward and downward disturbances in the balance of payments.

Moreover, the explicit intention of the present study is to provide *qualitative*, rather than quantitative, inferences about policy reactions. Thus, for instance, the investigation will seek to learn whether the discount rate is raised or lowered (or not changed at all) at times of balance-of-payments deficits, rather than how much it changes in response to a deficit of a given size.

As a device for suggesting hypotheses about policy reactions, subperiods of imbalances of payments are first distinguished. The unit of observation for a study of policy reactions to balance-of-payments dis-

[3] See G. L. Reuber, "The Objectives of Canadian Monetary Policy, 1949–61: Empirical 'Trade-offs' and the Reaction Function of the Authorities," *Journal of Political Economy*, April 1964, pp. 109–132; and William G. Dewald and Harry G. Johnson, "An Objective Analysis of the Objectives of American Monetary Policy, 1952–61," in Deane Carson (ed.), *Banking and Monetary Studies*, Homewood, Ill., 1963, pp. 171–189. A study devoted specifically to the length of the time lags which are involved in policy reactions (as well as the lags between the taking of policy measures and their impact upon the economy) is Albert Ando, E. Cary Brown, Robert M. Solow, and John Kareken, "Lags in Fiscal and Monetary Policy," in *Stabilization Policies*, Commission on Money and Credit, Englewood Cliffs, N.J., 1963, pp. 1–163. Interesting information about the time lags in policy reactions is contained in another recent study, reflecting opinions about policy processes in approximately the same countries which are investigated in the present study. See E. S. Kirschen *et al.*, *Economic Policy in Our Time*, Amsterdam, 1964, particularly Tables X.2 to X.5, pp. 274–276.

turbances is the time period during which the balance of payments is continuously in deficit, or continuously in surplus. The term "continuously" should be interpreted in a liberal way: a divergence in the direction of movement which occurs for a rather short time should not be regarded as starting a new period, but as a random discrepancy which may be disregarded. Needless to say, any such dissection of time into periods involves some element of arbitrariness in determining precisely the points at which each period starts and terminates, but this element will most often be rather slight.

The statistical investigation starts, then, with the observation of relationships among movements of policy and target indicators within each period. Had these periods been of very short duration, this procedure would hardly have been justified, for the same reasons that apply to observations of individual quarters: the movement of policy variables in any period is as likely to be a reaction to movements of target variables in earlier periods as to developments of the current one. Usually, however, the units of observation are considerably longer. Periods defined in the way suggested here normally last from two quarters to a number of years.

It may be assumed that when periods are of that length, policies within each period are normally a reaction to developments within the period rather than earlier. If this assumption is valid, an observation of concurrent changes in target and instrument variables would, indeed, reveal causal effects of target changes on policies. It must be recognized, however, that this is an assumption which, while probably reasonable, is supported more by casual observations, statements of policy makers, and general beliefs than by any firm analysis. Moreover, the procedure adopted here would be justified only if it could be assumed that policy measures do not have a great enough immediate impact on the target to reverse the direction of change which originally gave rise to the policy action: if this is not so, associations of changes in target and policy variables are more likely to reveal the effects of policies on targets than those of targets on policies. In other words, this procedure requires that the "inside lag" (or "recognition lag") be materially shorter than the "outside lag." There can, of course, be no assurance that this assumption is generally valid; and it must be recognized that whenever it does not hold true, the outcome of the present procedure may be doubtful. A related, somewhat similar, problem will be discussed later in this chapter.[4]

Where balance-of-payments disturbances follow a pattern approximating cyclical movements, this method of establishing relationships among variables will be complemented by the reference cycle analysis developed for the study of business cycles.[5] In this case, the turning points in the balance of payments will serve as the "reference

[4] The time-lag problem is touched upon in the aforementioned studies of Nurkse and Bloomfield. Both used annual data (and the year as a unit of observation) to analyze the relationship between two variables: the central bank's domestic assets and its foreign assets. Thus Nurkse wrote: "Our observations relate to yearly intervals. It is possible that domestic assets may be adjusted in the same direction as changes in international assets, not immediately, but with a lag of more than a year, in which case the year-to-year figures might conceal a process of adjustment taking place on the traditional lines. A lag in the process of adjustment is, after all, natural. Suppose an expansion of domestic credit gets under way in some country; the central bank's domestic assets increase while its international reserve is likely to fall, thus 'offsetting' part at least of the rise in domestic assets. It may be only after some time—say two or three years—that the central bank is 'pulled up short' by the fall in its international reserve and that it may feel obliged to start contracting its domestic assets; and this contraction, again, may go on for two or three years and is likely to be accompanied by a return flow of gold and exchange reserves. In both the expansion and the contraction phase, domestic and international assets may thus move in opposite directions from year to year, and yet the 'rules of the game' may operate, albeit with a lag." (*International Currency Experience*, pp. 68–70.)

Similarly, Bloomfield said: "The period of a year that is the basis of our comparison is essentially an arbitrary one that may conceivably conceal the fact that domestic assets *did* move more frequently in the same direction with international assets than in the opposite direction, but with a lag of more than one year." *Monetary Policy*, p. 50.

Nurkse and Bloomfield were worried by the possibility that central banks reacted with a lag of a few years. From all available evidence, this does not seem to be a matter of grave concern. Normally, central banks would probably react within a fairly short time—certainly, it could be expected, less than a year. If they do not, this would be an indication not of a slow machinery of response but of an intentional policy, which should by no means be described as following some "rules" with a time lag. Nurkse himself appears to suggest as much, in the sentence just following those quoted: "It is not always easy to draw the line between such delayed adjustment and deliberate neutralization with a view to avoiding adjustment." (*International Currency Experience*, p. 70.)

A much more important reason for the inadequacy of the use of annual data would seem to me to be that a period as long as a whole year is most likely to contain movements in opposite directions (in each variable) rather than a uniform movement, and the averaging of these movements must detract seriously from the validity of the investigation. Observations based on annual averages and on the year as a unit of investigation are thus likely to be of a limited significance. The only case in which this is less important is where the dominant movements took the form of rather long cycles, with a considerable number of years within each stretch of the cycle.

[5] See Arthur F. Burns and Wesley C. Mitchell, *Measuring Business Cycles*, New York, National Bureau of Economic Research, 1947, particularly Chapter 2.

dates." In principle, this method should yield essentially the same conclusions as that of observing subperiods of disturbances, since each such subperiod will be approximately—although not precisely—a phase of the reference cycle. This additional method of investigation may help in revealing the degree of consistency of each relationship. It may also uncover typical time lags between disturbances and reactions, when such typical lags exist.

Conclusions derived from these observations would, to repeat, be tentative. If an instrument (or policy) variable appears to move consistently in the direction required for balance-of-payments adjustment, it will be necessary to test whether this association may not be due to the consistent association of balance-of-payments fluctuations with the movements of another target variable, with which the changes of the instrument variable on hand are genuinely associated. Also, when instrument variables are seen not to move consistently with the balance of payments, or even to move consistently in a direction opposite to the requirements for balance-of-payments adjustment, this will require explanation. A few complementary methods of investigation will be used to deal with these problems. Thus the possibility of an association of the movements of an instrument variable with those of an alternative target variable will be examined by looking at the latter during periods of a uniform movement of the former. This may also be done through the reference cycle analysis in two ways: first, by taking as reference dates the turning points in the movements of the policy *instrument* and examining movements of alternative target variables during these cycles; second, by determining reference dates according to turning points in the movement of a *target* variable and observing the movements of instrument variables along these cycles.

Isolating periods in which the latter targets and balance-of-payments equilibrium called for opposite policies would, of course, make it easier to distinguish reactions to balance-of-payments disturbances from responses to changes in other targets. Unfortunately—for this purpose, but not for policy makers!—the number of such episodes of clear conflict has been rather small in the countries represented in the present report. Although the small number of such cases observed prevents a formal separate investigation of these episodes, special attention will usually be drawn to them.

The combined use of all these methods should yield answers to the following questions: Which policy instruments were used for balance-of-payments adjustment? Which were not, or were even manipulated in an opposite way to balance-of-payments requirements? Why were the latter not used for balance-of-payments purposes; that is, what other policy targets might have prevented the use of these instruments for balance-of-payments requirements? The analysis should also be able to show consistent differences among chronological periods in each country; or consistent differences—if they exist—between periods in which a correction of downward disturbances is called for and periods in which upward disturbances had to be corrected.

By the nature of the study, the relationships revealed cannot usually be completely and definitely established. The number of observations in each country—recalling that the unit of observation is a period of more or less monotonic disturbances—is necessarily small. It may typically be not more than ten or twelve, and very often be considerably less. The conventional methods of verifying the significance of apparent relationships would thus be of very little help in the present instance.[6] Statements of conclusions must, then, involve an element of judgment, and findings would have to be treated as plausible implications of the evidence rather than as unchallengeable truths. But that is, in varying degree, the nature of any empirical proposition.

A further elaboration of a few details in the techniques of analysis, and a description of various shorthand symbols, will be found in the chapter devoted to the experience of Japan (Chapter 3). The reader is advised to refer to the study of Japan as, in part, an extension of the present exposition of methods.

4. Adjustment Policies: Individual Variables and Policy Patterns

In examining the policy reactions to imbalances of payments, a judgment must be made as to whether a given change in a policy variable is "adjusting"—that is, whether it has the nature of working toward relieving the imbalance—or, on the contrary, "disadjusting." This judgment has to be made on two different levels.

First, it may be asked whether the change in the policy variable, *in*

[6] This refers also to the test of "indexes of conformity," which is used in cyclical analysis. See the warning, *ibid.*, pp. 183–185.

and by itself, has an impact in an adjusting direction: if it does it will be termed "adjusting." Thus, when there is a downward disturbance any change which tends to reduce aggregate demand or lower prices is an "adjusting" change; this would include an increase of the discount rate, an increase of minimum-reserve ratios, a decline of central or commercial bank credit, and so on. Terming such a change "adjusting" does not necessarily imply that the entire process of which this change is a part will have an adjusting effect. For instance, the discount rate may be raised, but demand for commercial bank credit may increase too, swelling credit volume and thus augmenting the balance-of-payments disturbances; however, without the change in the discount rate, the deterioration would have been even stronger, and this is, therefore, an "adjusting" change in the discount rate.

Second, the pattern of behavior of the whole array of instruments combined must be evaluated. Within this framework, what was termed an "adjusting" change before may not be and vice versa. In other words, when the over-all pattern is examined, attention is focused on the magnitude of some crucial variable. If this variable changes in an adjusting direction, the policy pattern as a whole is adjusting. A change in another variable which was found to be disadjusting when examined in isolation may still be consistent with the adjusting change in the crucial variable. To cite a simple example: Suppose the crucial variable is deemed to be money supply; this variable could change in an adjusting direction even though credit supply—which is only one of the factors which create money—changes in a disadjusting direction. The disadjusting nature of the movements of credit supply, *when judged by themselves,* may then still be consistent with the adjusting nature of the monetary policy. Judging the pattern as a whole would thus require focusing attention on the "crucial" variable or variables. This, indeed, whether explicitly or implicitly, has always been the way adjustment policies have been analyzed.

It may be worthwhile to discuss one particular pattern at some length due to its historical importance and its potential for analysis: this is the model which came to be known as the "rules of the game" of the gold standard. The books of Ragnar Nurkse and Arthur I. Bloomfield, which are often quoted and referred to in the present study, assume a certain definition of these "rules" in their examination of the degree of adherence of central banks to the gold-standard "rules of the game." The definition was provided by Nurkse; Bloomfield seems to have followed it as a matter of convenience and for the purpose of comparability, although he does not appear to regard it as an exclusive definition.[7] Nurkse defined the "rules of the game" in the following way:

> Whenever gold flowed in, the central bank was expected to increase the national currency supply not only through the purchase of that gold but also through the acquisition of additional domestic assets, and similarly, when gold flowed out, the central bank was supposed to contract its domestic assets also. In this way the influence of gold movements on the domestic credit base was to be magnified, and magnified in accordance with the central bank's reserve ratio.[8]

The "crucial" policy variable is, by this definition, the magnitude of the central-bank's domestic assets. Only a few would be likely to accept this definition in the extreme form in which it appears here. The last sentence implies that the "rules" require central banks to maintain a constant reserve ratio, i.e., of their foreign assets to their liabilities (this would also imply a constant ratio of the central bank's foreign assets to its domestic assets). While central banks were very often—particularly before 1914—legally required to maintain reserve ratios in one form or another, these were merely *minimum* require ments. Central banks were not bound by law to treat these ratios as maximum ratios as well, and there are no indications that they regarded a stable (rather than a minimum) reserve ratio as a guideline for their policy. Apparently, Nurkse himself did not consider this part of his definition essential, since there is no mention of the banks' reserve ratios in his empirical examination of the behavior of central banks.

But even deleting the last sentence from the quotation in question, this definition does not seem to be very useful. Three grounds may be offered to justify a definition of the "rules": (a) that this definition was used explicitly by central bankers, or was commonly accepted during the period under consideration; (b) that the definition, while not being used in an explicit way, was implied by other principles which

[7] "The concept of the rules of the game, which, incidentally, was first developed in the *post*-1914 literature—indeed, as far as I know, the term itself was first used by Keynes in the early twenties—admits of several possible interpretations and has been used in several senses." (Bloomfield, *Monetary Policy*, p. 47.)

[8] Nurkse, *International Currency Experience*, p. 66.

are known (or believed) to have been followed by policy makers; or
(c) that the definition is empirically found to have served as a guideline for policy actions during the relevant period.

Let us now examine the definition in question on these grounds.
It does not seem to be justified by the first criterion: the evidence offered by eminent students of the classical gold-standard period suggests that central bankers did not explicitly use such a definition, nor
was it commonly accepted or understood by them. On the last ground,
Nurkse's definition would have to be rejected on the basis of his own
evidence as well as that of Bloomfield. Nurkse himself found that the
"rules" were not actually followed in policy making in the interwar
years and Bloomfield found that they were not followed in the "classical" period either. We are left, thus, with the second ground. On this
ground the definition in question should again be rejected, and an alternative definition could be formed along the following lines.

The accepted principle of central banking during the classical gold-
standard era was, presumably, the maintenance of a stable international financial system; that is, a system free from (major) shifts in
foreign exchange rates and any form of state interference in the conduct of international transactions. Such a system cannot be viable if
countries lose all their gold and foreign exchange reserves. Any movement of reserves from one country to the other would thus have to be
checked before the losing country's reserves are depleted. According
to the theory of the day this was to be accomplished by two factors:
(1) the "price-specie-flow" mechanism; and (2) the effect of interest
rate variations on international short-term capital movements. The
proper functioning of the latter factor would require the manipulation of discount rates (or open-market operations) in an adjusting direction. The operation of the former mechanism would require that
the reserve-losing country experience a downward movement of its
money supply, and the gaining country an upward movement. In
Nurkse's words: "The gold standard, or indeed any system of stable
exchange rates, is a system in which the quantity of money in each
country is determined primarily by the balance of payments." [9] It is
an open question, however, how much the money supply should
change in each country. The more it changes, the faster the adjust-

[9] Nurkse, *International Currency Experience*, p. 67.

ment process will be. But certainly no one would expect this rule to require a rapid approach of the money supply to zero in the losing country, and to infinity in its partner. Even the most orthodox holders of the view that money is but a "veil" were probably aware of the difficulties created by changes in money supply, at least beyond a certain point or pace. There must be, therefore, some "proper" change (or rate of change) of the money supply. And there is no reason to suppose that this "proper" magnitude is necessarily proportionate to the change in foreign exchange reserves. Moreover, where foreign exchange reserves are considerable in relation to money supply, it may well be that a change of a given proportion in these reserves will in itself, by its direct effect, change money supply more than the central bank may deem proper for the necessary adjustment. In this situation, the central bank may act to offset part of this direct effect without feeling that it in any way violates some "rules of the game." The implication for the discount rate, however, is still clear. Since the end result for the reserve-losing country should be some fall of the quantity of money, interest rates must rise. Raising the discount rate serves this purpose and is particularly efficient where (as in the classical case of Britain) other interest rates traditionally follow discount rate movements directly and immediately.

If this view is accepted, the "crucial" variables become money supply and the discount rate, rather than domestic assets of the central bank. In the light of these remarks, it may be rewarding to examine the issue of "automatic stabilization," to which Nurkse paid much attention. He commented:

Whenever an inverse correlation is observed between a central bank's international and domestic assets, it may be quite wrong to interpret it as a deliberate act of neutralization on the part of that bank. It may well be due to the bank's inaction rather than to its action. An inflow of gold, for instance, tends to result in increased liquidity on the domestic money market, which in turn may naturally lead the market to repay some of its indebtedness to the central bank. The balance-sheet of the bank will show an increase in gold and a decrease in domestic discounts and advances, and so the gold movement will have been neutralized at least in part, even though the bank may have been completely passive. Similarly, an outflow of gold, tending to reduce the funds available to the market, may be partly offset by an increase in borrowing from the central bank on the market's initiative. Even to prevent domestic assets from changing in this way whenever gold flows in or out, would require definite action by the central bank either through changes in the terms of its lending or through sales or purchases of securities designed to offset the automatic responses in the market's indebtedness to the bank. To make domestic assets change in a manner *parallel* to changes in the international reserve would obviously demand a still greater degree of activity on the part of the central bank. Failing such action, "automatic neutralization" may tend to be the rule rather than the exception.[10]

According to the interpretation of the "rules of the game" previously suggested, it no longer follows that the "rules" not only require the central bank to act to offset this tendency of the commercial banks but even to effect "a still greater degree of activity." In certain instances, where the direct decline in the economy's liquidity due to the fall of foreign exchange reserves is regarded as too small for the proper functioning of the price-specie-flow mechanism, such activity would indeed be required. In other instances, the "rules" may induce the central bank to offset only part of the "automatic neutralization." In still other cases, no offsetting by the central bank may be required at all. Moreover, if the direct decline of money supply is deemed larger than "proper," the central bank may even be directed by the "rules" to encourage some creation of money from domestic sources; that is, the central bank may be called upon not only not to offset the "automatic neutralization" of commercial banks, but even to act on its own initiative in the same direction, so that an expansion of commercial bank credit would *partly* offset the effect of the fall of foreign exchange reserves on money supply.

It is thus clear that, following this interpretation of the "rules of the game," the attempt to examine compliance with the "rules" by observing correlations of movements of domestic and foreign assets of the central bank would have to be abandoned. When foreign assets fall, the "rules"—according to this interpretation—would generally accept either an increase or a decline of the central bank's domestic assets. All that the "rules" require is that the quantity of money decrease in the reserve-losing country and interest rates rise; and vice versa in the gaining country.[11]

[10] *Ibid.*, p. 70.

[11] For comments along roughly the same lines see R. Triffin, "National Central Banking and the International Economy," *Review of Economic Studies*, No. 36, 1946–47, pp. 53–75, particularly pp. 54–58.

The classical "rules of the game" have been discussed here in some detail mainly because the mode of behavior prescribed by them may still be expected to play a large role in policy making of central banks. But it is, of course, entirely possible that other models serve as a guide for policy. Thus, it is possible that the government may regard just the discount rate, or just money supply as a crucial variable, and not both. It may even disregard both, and attach crucial importance to the availability of credit; or it may pay little attention altogether to purely monetary variables and rely primarily on manipulation of the government's excess demand. While the present study does not intend to discuss the merits of such alternative models—either on a priori grounds or on the basis of the experience investigated—it will consider what model, or what variable, assumed to be crucial, could explain any consistent pattern of reactions which may be revealed.

The investigation of each individual country will thus consist of a discussion on two levels. First, each policy variable will be examined separately to see if, by itself, it reveals any consistent adjusting behavior, or the opposite. Then, by way of summary and interpretation, the observations of individual instruments will be combined to see whether they imply any typical pattern of reactions, and whether this pattern may be expected, in accordance with any reasonable model, to be of an adjusting nature. These discussions of individual countries will be preceded in each case by a section which will indicate, on the basis of prior information, what the major instruments used in the country are and the specific attributes of each instrument in that country, where this seems necessary for an understanding of the policy mechanism.

5. Selection of Policy Instruments

The selection of policy instruments, or variables, for observation will depend on the circumstances of each country. Differences in structure, law, and tradition lead to the use of different instruments in different countries. Here, statements of policy makers and of other analysts may be helpful as guidelines for experimentation. If, for instance, the magnitude of "secondary liquidity" is claimed to be of concern to the central bank of a certain country, this magnitude may be investigated in the study of that country; in another country this variable would be ignored, but the yield of government debt instruments might be studied; and so on.

In addition to having been judged, from prior information, to offer some promise of relevance, policy instruments will have to meet two criteria to be included in a systematic study. First, they must be subject to at least rough quantification. This requirement rules out certain policy instruments which are used for balance-of-payments adjustment. Direct control of imports is an important example: although these restrictions (and their relaxation) have often been used to affect the balance of payments, a quantitative measure of this variable is hard to come by, and this instrument will be ignored. This is true also of tariff duties: the size of individual duties can usually be verified, but calculations of "average" tariff levels are rare and of doubtful validity.

The other criterion which policy instruments must meet to be included is that of continuous and systematic use. Since the purpose of the study is to reveal a pattern—or even a change in pattern over time—policies which belong to just one episode must be omitted even if they can be quantified. Thus, for instance, if measures such as intervention in the forward exchange market or taxing capital movements were applied for a very few years of the total period, they cannot be the subject of a study of a general policy pattern.

It will be clear, then, that the present study by no means purports to describe and analyze the full array of instruments and measures used for balance-of-payments adjustment. It will attempt a systematic analysis only of policy instruments whose size can be measured and which have been used frequently, rather than in single episodes. In fact, as has been stated earlier, this means the major monetary and fiscal instruments which are intended primarily to affect aggregate demand. The present study is thus confined to analyzing the use of financial policies for balance-of-payments adjustment.[12] During most of the period studied, however, these policies were probably the most

[12] To use the terminology recommended by Machlup, the study covers, by and large, the instruments used for "real adjustment," to the exclusion of instruments used for "compensatory corrections." See Fritz Machlup, "Adjustment in International Payments," in Baldwin *et al.*, *Trade, Growth, and the Balance of Payments* (Essays in Honor of Gottfried Haberler), Amsterdam, 1965, pp. 185–213.

important instruments used for balance-of-payments adjustment in the countries in question.

A few instruments are common to most of the countries under investigation. These include the following: the discount rate, reserve-ratio requirements, open-market operations, central bank lending to the commercial banks, central bank lending to the government, central bank total domestic claims, commercial bank lending to the public, the money supply, government revenues, government expenditures, and the government's budgetary balance. Most of these variables require no comment; but some may deserve a few words of explanation.

Central Bank Lending to the Government.[13] This magnitude is calculated on a *net* basis; that is, it represents the size of the net indebtedness (either positive or negative) of the government to the central bank—derived by subtracting government deposits at the central bank from its borrowing from the bank. Central bank credit to the government increases the amount of liquidity in the economy only when it is net lending. Suppose the government is granted a loan from the bank but does not make any use of the receipts of its borrowing. This would be reflected in an increase in the government's deposits at the central bank equivalent in size to the loan. The loan does not affect the economy's liquidity at all; and this fact would be truly reflected in the size of the government's net indebtedness to the central bank, which would remain unchanged. To cite another example: the economy's liquidity would be affected in exactly the same way whether the government finances a given amount of spending by a loan from the central bank or by drawing upon existing deposits at the central bank. Again, the government's net indebtedness to the bank would be increased in exactly the same amount by these two alternative methods. These examples demonstrate the general point that the contribution of the government's transactions to the liquidity of the banking system should be measured not by the gross term but by the amount of *net* central bank lending to the government.

[13] When used in a general way, the term "government" will refer, in this study, to all official policy-making agencies; specifically, it will include the central bank. But in discussions of the central bank vs. the "government," the latter should obviously be interpreted in a narrower way—excluding the monetary authorities.

Purchases of government securities by the central bank in the open market would increase the amount of the government's gross and net indebtedness to the bank, while sales in the open market would reduce it. The effect on commercial bank liquidity is, indeed, identical whether the central bank purchases a newly issued government bond direct from the government—provided the latter spends the proceeds—or whether the bank buys in the market an existing government bond. Where the central bank is in effect committed to buy government securities from commercial banks, on given terms—as, for instance, in the U.S. before the "accord" of 1951—there may indeed be little meaning in separating the effect of open-market operations from that of direct transactions between the central bank and the government. In other instances—the U.S. since the early 1950's is probably a classic example—open-market operations are clearly decided upon at the discretion of the central bank and are used as an important instrument of monetary policy. In these instances, open-market operations would be recognized as a separate variable, while changes in the government's net indebtedness to the central bank would exclude variations in the amount of government paper at the central bank which are due to open-market operations.

Central Bank Total Domestic Claims. Changes in this variable are usually primarily a combination of changes in three other variables which are recorded separately: central bank lending to the commercial banks; central bank lending to the government; and open-market operations. But they may also reflect other components, such as central bank lending to the public (other than commercial banks). It should also be noticed that, in line with the previous argument, central bank lending to the government appears in this total on a *net* basis. The "total" of domestic claims is thus a hybrid in which some components are gross while one is net.[14]

[14] As was mentioned in the preceding section, Nurkse and Bloomfield attached primary importance to this variable of the central bank's total domestic claims in their studies. They took into account gross, rather than net, claims of the central bank on the government. The gap between the gross and net magnitudes may not have been of major importance frequently; but at least in one instance, for France in the late 1920's, it must have been significant according to Nurkse's own evidence. Nurkse noted, on this occasion: "To the extent that neutralization occurred through the growth of government deposits at the central bank, it cannot, of course, be observed from a mere comparison of the Bank's international and domestic assets." (*International Currency Experience*, p. 77.)

The Government's Revenues, Expenditures, and Budgetary Balance.
In the fiscal sphere, the major policy tool which one might expect to
be employed for purposes of balance-of-payments adjustment is probably an over-all (surplus or deficit) balance of the budget. This may
best be discussed in terms of the government's "excess demand" for
goods and services.[15] An increase in the government's excess demand—
whether an increase in a deficit, a reduction of a surplus, or a shift
from a surplus to a deficit—is a contribution to the economy's aggregate demand, and thus an inflationary measure; and a reduction of
excess demand is the opposite. The investigation will thus examine
not the position of the government's balance (i.e., whether it is a
surplus or a deficit) but the *direction of change* in the balance from
one period to the other.

It may also be interesting to look separately at the changes in government revenues and government expenditures. If the government
does manipulate its excess demand in reaction to balance-of-payments
disturbances, this observation may show which tool is used for that
purpose; that is, whether it is mainly revenues which are changed or
expenditures, or possibly the two in opposite directions or different
proportions.

In a statistical study of this type, it is inevitably the *ex post* realized
movements of each policy variable which are taken into account.
These movements may, however, differ from the *ex ante* changes—the
realized movement is not necessarily identical with the one intended
by the policy maker. This difficulty almost certainly increases in importance with the complexity of the process by which the policy variable in question is brought into play.

Monetary variables differ as to the directness with which they can
be manipulated by the monetary authority. On the one hand, such
variables include instruments which are controlled directly and precisely by the authority, like the discount rate, minimum-reserve requirements, or open-market operations. On the other hand, they in-

---

[15] The "excess demand" is the excess of the government's expenditures on goods
and services over those of its revenues which reduce the public's disposable income.
In effect, the expenditures include very often loans to other organizations (whether
private or nationalized), the case for whose inclusion as an element in the government's "excess demand" is not clear. Also, the data actually used refer to cash
budgets, while the use of accrual budgets—had they been available—might be argued
to be more appropriate.

clude a variable such as money supply, which is affected by the monetary authority only through a complex and long drawn out chain of reactions. It is continuously affected by exogenous, autonomous changes, not all of which are immediately taken into account. In between are variables such as components of the central bank's assets, or the supply of credit, which are at various stages of remove from the direct action of the monetary authority. It may be debated at what stage a variable is too little affected to be an "instrument" in monetary policy.[16] The advantage of examining variables at different levels, as in the present study, is that it makes possible an analysis, as has been explained in the preceding section, which is not tied in advance to the investigation of one specific model.

This problem may be even more relevant for budgetary policies: the identification of realized, *ex post* magnitudes with *ex ante* policies might well be questioned. Thus a realized reduction in the govern-

---

[16] Challenged by a similar problem of determining what could be instruments of monetary policy, Kareken and Solow stopped somewhat earlier on this road. They argue: "It is not true, except in some irrelevant long-run sense, to say that the Federal Reserve controls either M [money supply] or its rate of change. What the Federal Reserve can do is buy and sell in the open market, set reserve requirements, and set the discount rate. A little less directly . . . we may say that the authorities control the effective primary reserves of the commercial banks . . . and at one further remove we may say that the measure of monetary policy is the power of the banking system to carry earning assets. This is what the monetary authorities do. They do not move a pointer on a dial marked M or even ΔM." (John Kareken and Robert M. Solow, "Lags in Monetary Policy," Part I of "Lags in Fiscal and Monetary Policy," *Stabilization Policies,* pp. 17–18.)

Later, however, the authors state: "Why stop, though, with the assumptions (or attributions of knowledge) so far suggested? Why stop, that is, with Max E [maximum earning assets of commercial banks] as the instrument variable? Why not continue making assumptions until the ultimate policy variables, the price level, the rate of unemployment, etc., emerge as the instrument variables of the Federal Reserve? Above it was suggested that the System can be regarded as knowing how the direct determinants of total member bank reserves are themselves determined, and as being able to predict future values of the arguments of these functions which it does not set. But then why not assume in addition that the System knows member banks' demand for excess reserves, in which case it can be regarded as setting actual as well as maximum earning assets. And with a few more assumptions, the system can be regarded as setting the price level.

"Evidently, there is no basis in logic for stopping at one point rather than another—for making certain assumptions rather than others . . ." (*Ibid.,* p. 81).

Indeed, with no basis in logic, the definition of instruments or the "assumptions" we make may change from time to time and from one country to another. As stated in the text, an advantage of always considering instruments on various "levels" is that it imposes fewer restrictions, by an investigator, on the assumed mode of behavior of the policy maker.

ment's excess demand in this investigation represents a contractive policy, and a realized increase, an expansionary policy. It may be argued that this is a particularly dubious procedure in this sphere; that, for instance, when the government undertakes an expansionary policy—say, by reducing tax rates without changing expenditures—the ensuing expansion may lead to a budgetary surplus through its effect on the amount of tax revenues. Identifying a budgetary surplus with a contractive policy would be entirely misleading in this instance.

Such a contradiction between intended and realized budgetary balance—due merely to induced changes rather than to autonomous changes in exogenous variables—would not be possible under the "textbook" assumptions of multiplier analysis. Specifically, it would not be possible when *ex ante* investment is held constant, or even assumed to be a function of income. Under different assumptions, however, this contradiction is conceivable. It could be produced, for instance, by an "acceleration principle," or by assuming investment to be a function of *tax rates,* whether in general or certain corporate tax rates.

Ideally, the anticipated budgetary balance should have been used rather than the realized balance. However, this cannot be achieved in practice. At best, estimates of this magnitude are available for a fiscal year as a whole; even then, they do not necessarily reflect fully the anticipations of policy makers. Estimates of planned budgets would be of only little use for the purpose of this study. It is hoped that the adoption of budgetary performance as a substitute for expected budgetary magnitudes will not bias the results seriously. This hope may be justified when the periods of observation are not unduly long—say, not more than a year or a year and a half. Within short periods, changes induced by measures taken during the period may be expected to be slight in comparison with the primary changes. Thus, the danger that realized magnitudes will give indications contrary to those of intended policies is probably small when the period is short. When partial, circumstantial evidence on the government's intentions is available, this information will be indicated.

Unlike the monetary area, the study of fiscal policy is confined here to the "ultimate" variables. It considers the government's over-all balance in its budget; one step below, it observes the two components of the budget—revenues and expenditures. But there it stops. It does not

analyze the means by which each of these components is, in turn, affected—means which could well be considered policy variables in their
own right. This treatment of the fiscal area results from the practical
limitations of the investigation. It is easy to tell how the discount rate
or the minimum-reserve ratio were changed during a given period. It
would be immensely more difficult to say how the "tax rate" changed.
This "tax rate" is some weighted average of a myriad of individual
tax rates, many of which may move in opposite directions in a given
period and certainly in different proportions. Even the study of entire
categories of these rates, e.g., excise duties or income taxes, would be
extremely complicated. A component such as the personal income tax
would in itself raise serious problems: it is a whole structure, not all
parts of which may move always in the same direction. In a study of
the present scope, any attempt to observe such "partial" variables in
a systematic manner must be abandoned.

It may seem odd that the foreign exchange rate, which is presumably a major policy instrument among balance-of-payments adjustment policies, is not mentioned among the policy variables in this
study. The reason for this is, of course, quite simple: in the countries
and during the period under investigation, changes in foreign exchange
rates were almost entirely absent. These changes were confined to a
few episodes in France and one each in Germany and the Netherlands
and offer no basis for systematic analysis. The present study is thus
defined beforehand, in practice, as an investigation of balance-of-payments adjustment policies under fixed exchange rates.

The important exception to this pattern in the Group of Ten is
Canada, which had a fluctuating rate during most of the period. Although the study of Canada promises to be of considerable interest in
its own right, Canada's deviation from the general pattern makes it
less useful as an ingredient in international comparisons and a study
of international policy patterns. For this reason, Canada has been excluded from the present study.

6. Identification of Balance-of-Payments Disturbances

Since the study's purpose is to identify and examine the reactions of
governments to balance-of-payments disturbances through their policy measures, the variable or variables which would be required,

ideally, to indicate disturbances are those which serve this purpose in the decision making process of the government concerned. The lack, however, of direct information about these "ideal" variables makes it necessary to substitute the researcher's judgment for that of the government concerned and to experiment with alternative variables. Since circumstances vary from one country to another, there should be no attempt to determine a single exclusive principle for identifying disturbances in all the countries studied. Where no particular special circumstances are apparent, however, it would be a good rule to stick as closely as possible to commonly accepted principles of identifying disturbances, since these are likely to be adhered to by the government concerned. It should be obvious from these remarks that it may be necessary to experiment with more than one definition or principle, even in the case of a single country.

The variable which appears to be the simplest, most easily observed, and most frequently available, is the country's external reserves. An upward movement of these reserves would indicate an upward disturbance, or a "surplus"; while a downward movement would be a downward disturbance, or a "deficit." The category selected to represent this variable is that of gross official reserves. The definition of this series usually includes holdings of gold and of foreign exchange by the central bank or government plus the net IMF position.

Holdings of foreign exchange by commercial banks, on the other hand, are probably not usually counted by the government as part of the reserves for the purpose on hand. Before the era of convertibility, banks in most countries were normally allowed to hold abroad only necessary working balances. In later years, commercial banks have presumably been guided by their own initiative and considerations in determining the amount of their foreign exchange holdings. They do not act as agents of the central authorities; their holdings (and indebtedness), and changes in them, are thus presumably disregarded in the government's identification of imbalances of payments.[17] Yet when commercial bank holdings are substantial, it may be worthwhile to experiment with including them in the country's reserves, for the purpose of determining episodes of balance-of-payments disturbances. In

---

[17] This approach is similar to that taken for the United States by the Bernstein Committee. See Report of the Review Committee, *Balance of Payments Statistics of the United States: A Review and Appraisal*, Washington, D.C., 1965, Chapter 9.

the countries covered by the present report, this inclusion seemed, usually, to affect the analysis very little.

Another series which has been experimented with is that of balance-of-payments surpluses and deficits as defined by the Balance-of-Payments Division of the International Monetary Fund.[18] It covers the period from 1958 onward, and uses the "official settlements" concept: "A surplus or deficit is defined as the balance of all transactions other than 'official settlements' (i.e., excluding changes in official gold and foreign exchange assets, in net IMF positions, and in liabilities to foreign monetary authorities, and adjusted for advance repayments of foreign debt by governments). The over-all surplus or deficit so defined is equal to the basic balance, unrecorded transactions, and all movements of short-term capital, excluding only those that constitute official settlements." [19] This definition thus includes not only changes in a country's reserves but also changes in its liabilities to foreign monetary authorities and advance repayments of foreign debt by governments. The two series usually demonstate a very high degree of agreement in direction of imbalances, and most often also in their intensity, during the period covered by the two (that is, from 1958 onward).

In some cases, it may be advisable to experiment with still other variables. For instance, a government may view only an imbalance of the current account as a "disturbance," while disregarding movements on capital account. If this is suspected, the representation of disturbances by deficits or surpluses on current account may be rewarding.

Still another variable which may have to be taken into account is the *level* of reserves. A situation may occur where the government wishes to see a change in reserves—an accumulation or, probably much less often, a reduction. The government would not then consider any change in reserves as a "disturbance" but any discrepancy between the desired level of reserves and their actual level; or, in other words, a change not commensurate with the change desired by the government. The determination of a "desired level" is, of course, not an easy task. When the level of reserves has been constant over the long run, it may be assumed that a shortfall of reserves below this level could be considered a downward disturbance even when reserves

18 This information was kindly provided by the Division.
19 *International Monetary Fund,* 1965 Annual Report, p. 66.

are rising (from a particularly low level), and vice versa. When reserves domonstrate a long-term movement, some form of determining their trend would be required, and the assumption that the "trend level" is the desired one may be attempted.

Most of the experiments that could be made will probably not be required. Two guidelines will help to indicate the need for experimentation: first, an explicit statement of policy makers, or of other analysts, that a certain variable is used to measure balance-of-payments disturbances—in which case the variable in question would merit an investigation; second, a lack of definite conclusions when the simple variable of foreign exchange reserve holdings is analyzed.

The problem arising from the substitution of *ex post* for *ex ante* magnitudes, which has been pointed out in the discussion of policy variables, is just as relevant to the definition of targets in general, and to the specific target of balance-of-payments equilibrium. The study investigates relationships among *realized* movements of variables. *Anticipations,* on the other hand, are entirely absent from this examination. In the government's "reaction function," manipulations of policy variables will in effect be related to the present stock and the anticipated, future flow of each magnitude that represents a target variable. Past flows enter into the function only as a factor which affects these two. The statistical investigations can, in principle, take account of present stocks; this will indeed be done as has just been mentioned: the level of foreign exchange reserves will be introduced whenever it seems to be a promising addition to the analysis. Anticipations, on the other hand, are replaced by the statistically observable flows which, in relation to each point of time in which a policy measure is undertaken, have either taken place in the past or will have been realized in effect in the future. This is certainly not a perfect substitute, but it is probably the best available. A conceivable alternative would be to construct each government's "anticipation function," and derive from it anticipated values for the target variables. This procedure might possibly be attempted, but it is certainly not feasible in this study.

If it is found that the government does not react to "disturbances" in the balance of payments in a way which would adjust them, this could be the result of either of two factors. First, the government may refrain from an adjustment policy because the policy would have, in the government's judgment, an undesirable impact on other targets. And second, the government may be indifferent to the so-called disturbance or may even actually welcome it. The double meaning of the term "disturbance" should therefore be clarified. As used in this study, "disturbance" does not necessarily indicate that the government so regarded the development in question. The attempt to achieve a certain level of reserves, which has just been mentioned, is an important illustration of this point. If a level of reserves higher than the existing one is considered a target, then not an accumulation of reserves but its absence would be regarded, by the government, as a "disturbance." It should therefore be emphasized that the use of this term does *not* necessarily imply an expression of the government's view: on the contrary, one of the outcomes of the study could be, to identify what the government actually considered a disturbance by examining the government's policies. Yet, it is just as important to keep in mind that the study is intended to draw inferences for the international monetary system as a whole. For the latter, the accumulation of reserves by one country may be a "disturbance" even if it is not so regarded by that country. And it is, therefore, imperative to learn how that country reacted to such "disturbances."

7. *Alternative Policy Targets*

Policy targets may be of various kinds and shades, but most of them could certainly not be identified without intensive study. It would obviously not be feasible to try to secure information about all of these targets; and for the present purpose such an attempt would probably be unrewarding even if it were feasible. As explained earlier, other target variables were introduced in this study mainly to determine whether a policy pattern which appears to be a reaction to imbalances of payments can be explained instead by their movements. While the number of such explanations could be very large, it seems that the observation of a few "global" targets which are generally considered to share with the balance of payments a claim on some of the same policy instruments would go a considerable way toward satisfying the requirements of such an examination. These targets are maintenance of price stability, maintenance of full employment, and the achievement of a high, steady rate of growth.

The observation of the first two targets is relatively simple. The indexes of consumer prices and of wholesale prices appear to be used most often as indicators of movements of the general price level. Usually, although not always, these two indexes will yield similar results, particularly as far as substantial price movements are concerned. This is also true about measurements of unemployment. Although series such as registered unemployment and the number of unemployed projected from labor force surveys may differ significantly when absolute levels are concerned, indicated directions and intensities of changes will be largely similar.

The statistical representation of the target of the rate of growth is more complicated. This is, by its nature, a longer-term target. A measurement of developments during a given period will inevitably reveal the effect of (1) changes in the economy's productive resources and the productivity of these resources—which is, presumably, what the target of "growth" refers to—and (2) the rate of utilization of existing capacity, in which the rate of employment, considered as a separate target, is of crucial importance. The separation of actual performance into these components would clearly be beyond the scope of a study of this kind. The rate of growth will therefore have to be measured by some summary indication of the current performance of the economy, despite the limitations just noted.

Conceptually, the best available yardstick for measuring the economy's over-all performance would probably be the rate of increase of GNP (or NNP—the difference between the two will usually be slight). For a number of reasons, however, a measure conforming better to the purpose of this study is the rate of increase of industrial production. In the first place, it is usually available within a fairly short time, unlike the GNP estimates, which in most countries are available only with a considerable time lag. It may thus be assumed that, for the purpose of determining their short-term policies, governments which have this measurement available at the relevant time regard it as indicating the growth rate. The government may justly feel that this use is not likely to be very misleading, since industrial production is itself a major component of the national product in the countries concerned. Even aside from the advantage of being readily accessible, industrial production data often attract particular attention. Industrial production is more susceptible to the effects of short-term governmental policies—and reflects them better—than do other economic activities, and in particular those of the agricultural sector. Likewise, the industrial sector is often assigned a particularly heavy weight, e.g., in comparison with the services sector, by governmental observers. For these reasons, the index of industrial production will usually represent the growth target in the present study.

Beyond the problem of what statistical series best represent the various target variables, the question of how these series should be interpreted must be raised. It must be assumed that a given change (or position) of a series indicates a desirable movement (or level) for the target on hand; while another position is undesirable and calls for correction. The number of possible assumptions, i.e., of possible modes of governmental views, may again be very large. Thus, where the price stability target is concerned, any increase in the price level (measured, for example, by the consumer price index) may be regarded as a disturbance which should be corrected. But if a general upward trend of prices exists, it is possible that a price increase no greater than the average is not a source of concern; or that faster increases are not considered a disturbance as long as the price level is below its "trend line"; or, as still another possibility, that only increases in the rate of increase of prices are considered disturbances. A similar variety of models is conceivable when unemployment is examined. When the rate of unemployment is high in comparison with its average level, and rising, this would certainly be considered a disturbance. It is not clear, however, how a situation in which unemployment is high but falling would be regarded; or, to take the opposite combination, how a situation of low but rising unemployment should be treated. The same ambiguity holds when the growth target is examined. A situation where industrial production is both below its "trend line" and falling would, almost certainly, be regarded as a disturbance. The answer is not clear, however, when the rate of increase is above average, but production is still below its trend level, or when the rate of increase is falling, but production is above its trend level; and so on.

It would be next to impossible to try to examine all such possibilities. In any case, it should be recalled that the study does not purport to investigate *all* the possible targets, and cannot therefore be exhaustive. For this reason, only very few models of reaction will be examined. In general, it will be assumed that price stability is contravened when prices rise more rapidly than in recent experience; that the target of high employment is contravened by an increase in unemployment; and that a decline in the rate of increase of industrial production (and, needless to say, a negative rate) indicates a deterioration of the target of rapid growth. In the countries which have been investigated, it appears from casual observation that other reasonable models would most often have given similar indications about the timing of disturbances. In some cases where these indications are clearly contradictory, this will be taken into account informally. However, it should again be emphasized that it cannot be claimed that the result of this procedure is based on an exhaustive and definitive study of all reasonable possibilities. It is limited, as has been stated earlier, to the examination of a very limited number of the simplest, and probably most obvious, among these possible models.

3

JAPAN

1. Policy Instruments

MONETARY POLICY

Monetary policy is conducted primarily by the Bank of Japan in cooperation with, or subject to the approval of, the Ministry of Finance. Commercial banking institutions in Japan are of various types. Some are private, while others have been established and run by the government; some are of a general nature, while others fulfill specialized functions. There are no separate discount houses of the British type in Japan. The most important category of banks is that known as "All Banks," which in terms of the amount of loans or the size of deposits constitutes over 80 per cent of the commercial banking system. It consists of "City Banks," "Local Banks," "Trust Banks," and "Long-Term Credit Banks." Other categories of bank-type financial institutions are usually restricted in nature to rather narrow purposes. They include institutions such as agricultural or industrial cooperatives, credit associations, or investment corporations. Monetary policy is concerned by and large, although not exclusively, with the category of "All Banks"—where, in turn, it affects primarily the large (and heavily concentrated) "City Banks."

The following are the actual or potential instruments at the disposal of the Bank of Japan.

The Discount Rate. This is the major instrument used in the conduct of monetary policy in Japan. The rate, or rates, apply to bills discounted at the Bank of Japan and to advances against collateral from the Bank to commercial banks (there are usually no overdrafts on the Bank). These loans and discounts have been very important in Japan not only as a means of bridging temporary gaps in banks' reserves, as is customary elsewhere, but also as a major long-term (in effect) source of liquidity for the banking system. Since, as will be mentioned later, the government's budget has been approximately balanced for reasonably long periods of time and open-market operations are of minor importance, borrowing from the central bank is the only major source of additional banking liquidity beside the accumulation of foreign exchange reserves.

During most of the period, the Bank of Japan applied a system of multiple discount rates. This was known as the "higher-interest-rate system." Each bank was allocated a quota of loans from the Bank of Japan, for which a low "basic" discount rate was in force. Above this quota a higher rate—the "first penalty rate"—came into effect. Sometimes a second margin of Bank of Japan lending was established, beyond which a still higher rate—the "second penalty rate"—was applied. Until August 1955, the basic discount rate was of practically no significance for monetary policy: loans to all the banks considerably exceeded their rationed quotas so that the first penalty rates, and very often the second, were the relevant rates for marginal decisions. In August 1955, the basic rate was increased considerably and quotas were changed. From that date on, the basic rate became indeed the usually meaningful figure. Higher penalty rates were still applied even at later dates, but sparingly and in exceptional cases. In 1962, the system of "higher interest rates" was abolished altogether.

In addition to influencing the amount of banks' borrowing through changes in the discount rate, the Bank of Japan sometimes determines actual ceilings of the amounts lent to each individual bank. This is done in connection with rationing the credit granted by commercial banks to their customers, a practice which will be mentioned shortly.

Reserve Requirements. The minimum-reserve requirement instrument has been used only for the last few years and is still of minor significance. Traditionally, commercial banks in Japan have held practically no reserves beyond the cash used in day-to-day operations and small deposits at the Bank of Japan required for interbank clearing. In 1957, a law was passed which enabled the Bank of Japan to require the banks to hold reserves, in the form of deposits at the Bank of Japan, at a ratio not exceeding 10 per cent of the banks' deposits. In fact, reserve requirements were laid down for the first time in September 1959; the reserve ratios varied then according to the type of bank and the type of deposit, but they were all very low—around 1 per cent of bank deposits. Minimum-reserve ratios were slightly raised in October 1961 and again in December 1963; on the latter date, they reached .5 per cent of time deposits and 3 per cent of sight deposits. Apparently these increases, besides being slight, were not considered as monetary measures intended to affect current monetary developments. As a rule, reserve requirements have thus not played any significant role; although towards the end of 1965, a reduction of legal reserve ratios (to virtually zero) was undertaken apparently as a means of encouraging monetary expansion.

Open-Market Operations. The instrument of open-market operations, as this term is normally understood, was not employed in Japan until recent years. This has been attributed to a number of factors, chief of which were the lack of a substantial organized capital market and a low pegging of rates on government securities. Occasionally, the Bank of Japan conducted a transaction in securities with a commercial bank, but this was usually a bilateral, ad hoc transaction—with a specific bank, in a specific security, and for a specified period. It was usually motivated by the desire to bail the bank concerned out of a particular difficulty or, conversely, to provide it with an outlet for a particularly large accumulation of reserves. It was not used as an instrument of over-all monetary policy.

Towards the end of the period (since 1963), open-market operations became more significant in size and probably a more integral part of over-all monetary policy; they are still, however, conducted in a bilateral manner rather than strictly in the open market.

Direct Credit Control. The Bank of Japan has maintained, with varying degrees of severity, a direct control on the amount of credit granted by each individual bank. In general, this has been an important instrument, in fact, the only significant tool of monetary policy aside from discount rate manipulations. Naturally, the use of this control is limited to periods when the banks wish to expand their loans more than the Bank of Japan is willing to allow: It cannot be used to encourage an expansion of credit. By and large, therefore, this instrument was relevant primarily when the monetary authorities were trying to limit rather than encourage the expansion of credit.

The control system was adapted in its present form in 1954. It operates not on a formal, legal basis but through "moral suasion" by the Bank of Japan and is known as the "discount-window operation," or "official guidance." Despite its informal character, it is extensive and rather detailed, particularly with regard to the few large "City Banks," and the "Long-Term Credit Banks." The Bank of Japan, in consultation with the banks, determines—at least at certain periods—the amount of credits that each can extend to the public in a month's time; it sometimes follows the actual development of the banks' accounts on a day-by-day basis. The Bank of Japan imposes its views both by moral suasion and by pressure and sanctions, either threatened or actually practiced. Sanctions include primarily a restriction of the amount of Bank of Japan lending to the "delinquent" bank; or, insofar as the banking system as a whole is concerned, a threat that discount rates will be further increased if the "voluntary" control proves to be ineffective.

FISCAL POLICY

The central government's budget consists of various accounts. The most important among these is the general account, which encompasses most of the normal government activities, both of a current and of a capital nature. In addition, there are about forty special accounts. These have widely different functions, sources of income, and types of expenditure. Some of them channel savings accumulated by governmental saving institutions or by the social security system into capital expenditures. A major "special account," from the standpoint of size, is the foodstuffs control program, which is essentially a form of subsidization of mass-consumed (and mass-produced) foodstuffs, primarily rice. Another major special account is the foreign exchange account. Strictly speaking, the latter is not a legitimate part of the government's budget but a reflection of the movement of foreign exchange in the country's foreign transactions. In Japan, as frequently in other countries with foreign exchange control, these transactions are handled formally through the Treasury.

In principle, the government adheres to a balanced-budget policy, and has indeed maintained a balanced budget over the period as a whole and over any reasonably long fraction of it. Over short periods, deficits or surpluses do show up. As a rule, the general account provides a surplus, which is transferred to some of the special accounts, thus maintaining an over-all balance.

The budgetary procedure in Japan apparently does not allow a large measure of administrative flexibility. Supervision of the budgetary performance by the parliament (the Diet) is tight; rules are determined in advance for the annual budget without leaving much leeway in actual execution.

The government does not, as a rule, borrow much from the public (including the commercial banks). As mentioned earlier, interest rates on government bonds are pegged at a low level, considerably below comparable rates in the market. Likewise, the government does not normally deal in short-term borrowing from (or lending to) foreign countries. Budgetary cash surpluses and deficits are expressed, thus, mainly in changes in the government's indebtedness to the Bank of Japan.[1] The Bank is not restricted by law in its extension of credit to the government. It is, moreover, obligated to underwrite the government's short-term securities. The government itself, on the other hand, is legally denied the right to borrow at long term from the Bank of Japan or to sell long-term securities to it. In effect, the Bank of Japan's obligation to "underwrite" government securities implies that it has to actually buy these securities, since the public would not buy them under the conditions of their issuance; some securities are resold, however, to governmental agencies. In the earlier years of the period, a sizable portion of the government's indebtedness to the Bank of Japan took the form of loans. These later declined, and from about 1954 to 1961 loans to the government were nil or negligible in comparison with the amount of government bonds at the Bank. Since 1962, however, loans—this time in the form of debentures rather than advances—again became prominent.

2. Statistical Analysis

Data on changes in policy and target variables are presented in diagrammatic form in Chart 1. It appears that the series (not shown in the chart) of balance-of-payments surpluses and deficits since 1958 gives almost the same impression, so far as turning points in directions

---

[1] The word "cash" should be emphasized. "Accrued" obligations of the public to the government, or vice versa, are certainly widespread. It may also be mentioned that from time to time the government becomes indebted to commercial banks due to the latter's assumption of deferred government payments. For instance, food subsidies may first be paid out by commercial banks, which are later reimbursed by the government.

of movements are concerned, as the series of gold and foreign exchange reserves. It was therefore decided to take the latter—with minor modifications suggested by the former—as the indicator of balance-of-payments disturbances. An upward movement of this magnitude is considered an upward imbalance (that is, a balance-of-payments surplus); a downward movement, an imbalance in the opposite direction.

The period under review is divided, accordingly, into subperiods of upward disturbances, downward disturbances, or stability in the balance of payments. The classification of the period into subperiods appears in the first column of Table 1. In Chart 1, subperiods of downward disturbances are shaded by diagonal lines, subperiods of stability are shaded gray, and subperiods of upward disturbances are not shaded.

The remaining columns of Table 1 show the over-all trend of each of the policy variables considered during each subperiod of disturbance. For convenience of observation and exposition, each such movement is given a sign. It is marked by a plus sign when the movement of the variable complies with the assumption that the variable is manipulated in the direction required for balance-of-payments adjustment (for brevity, this will be referred to as an "adjusting direction"), by a minus sign when the variable moves in a direction opposite to that which balance-of-payments adjustment would require, and by an asterisk when the variable does not move, although balance-of-payments adjustment would have justified an upward or a downward movement.[2] It should be clear, in line with the discussion in the for-

---

[2] Similar use of plus and minus signs, in a context limited to the study of a single policy variable (the central bank's domestic assets), was made by Nurkse and by Bloomfield in their aforementioned studies. See Nurkse, *International Currency Experience*, pp. 68–70, and Bloomfield, *Monetary Policy under the Gold Standard*, pp. 47–51.

It should be emphasized—indeed, this point could not be overstressed—that the use of such signs in the present study (as, I believe, in its predecessors) does *not* have any normative connotation. Giving, for instance, a plus mark to a certain movement does by no means indicate that this movement is considered desirable in general, or by some particular yardstick, or that a different policy would be somehow less desirable. As was stated in the preceding chapters, the present study does not attempt to pass judgment on the appropriateness of policies pursued by various countries at various times. It does not intend to discuss the merits of various policy targets; and it does not purport to examine the issue—nor, a fortiori, to reach conclusions about it—of the adequacy of certain policy instruments for given policy targets. The present study is viewed as merely a necessary step on the road for such inquiries. Thus, if any convenient "neutral" symbols could be used for the purpose of identification, they would have been adopted. The plus and minus signs were selected because no other symbols are completely neutral, while these signs enjoy the advantages of having been used in distinguished and well-known precedents and of being visually convenient.

CHART 1

Japan: Time Series of Selected Variables

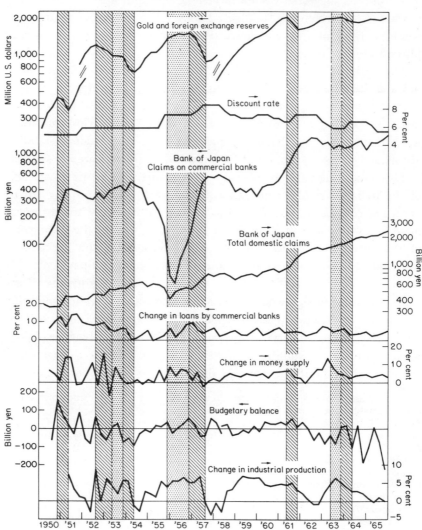

Note: Diagonal-line areas represent periods of downward imbalances; gray areas represent stability; and white areas represent upward imbalances.

· TABLE 1

Japan: Movements of Policy Variables During Subperiods of Disturbances

Subperiod	Gold and Foreign Exchange Reserves (indication of disturbance) (1)	Discount Rate (2)	Bank of Japan Claims on Commercial Banks (3)	Bank of Japan Total Domestic Claims (4)	Commercial Bank Lending to Public (rate of change) (5)	Money Supply (rate of change) (6)	Budgetary Balance (7)
II–IV 1950	rise	a	+ rise	* stable	n.a.	n.a.	surplus
IV 1950–II 1951	fall	a	– rise	– rise	– rises	– rises	* surplus
II 1951–III 1952	rise	a	* stable	+ rise	* stable	* stable	+ balanced
III 1952–II 1953	fall	a	– rise	– rise	* stable	– rises	– deficit
II–IV 1953	stable	a	stable	rise	stable	falls	deficit
IV 1953–II 1954	fall	a	– rise	– rise	+ falls	+ falls	* deficit
II 1954–IV 1955	rise	a	– fall	– fall	– falls	* stable	– balanced
IV 1955–IV 1956	stable	stable	rise	rise	stable	rises	surplus
IV 1956–III 1957	fall	+ raised	– rise	– rise	* stable	+ falls	– deficit
III 1957–II 1961	rise	+ reduced	* no trend	+ rise	* stable	* stable	* mostly balanced
II–IV 1961	fall	+ raised	– rise	– rise	* stable	+ falls	* moderate surplus
IV 1961–II 1963	rise	+ reduced	* no trend	+ rise	* stable	+ rises	+ mostly deficit
II–IV 1963	stable	stable	fall	rise	stable	stable	* mostly deficit
IV 1963–II 1964	fall	+ raised	– rise	– rise	+ falls	+ falls	* mostly deficit

Note: + indicates a movement in the direction required for balance-of-payments adjustment.
   – indicates a movement in the opposite direction.
   * indicates no movement or a very slight one.

ª not applicable.

mer chapter, that at this stage each variable is examined *by itself,* and not yet as part of the general pattern; and is judged according as it moves in an "adjusting" direction or not.

The stage is thus set for the observation of policy variables. If a variable moves consistently in the direction conforming to the need for balance-of-payments adjustment, it would be tentatively concluded that manipulation of this variable was indeed motivated by the purpose of adjustment. If no such consistent behavior is found— and, a fortiori, when a variable consistently behaves in the opposite fashion—it must be concluded that the variable under consideration did not serve as a tool of balance-of-payments adjustment.

Looking, first, at the discount rate (column 2 of Table 1), it is immediately apparent that this variable moved consistently—indeed, with no exception—in an adjusting direction: the rate was raised when a downward disturbance in the balance of payments took place, and lowered in opposite instances. The evidence thus suggests the tentative conclusion that discount rate policy was used by the Bank of Japan as an instrument of balance-of-payments adjustment.[3]

Next, in column 3 of Table 1, Bank of Japan lending to commercial banks is examined. Here a consistent pattern again appears, but in the opposite direction. These loans move regularly upward at times of a downward disturbance in the balance of payments, and vice versa; these are, of course, movements which would augment disturbances rather than correct them. In the few exceptions to this pattern the variable in question merely did not move, instead of moving in a disadjusting direction; only in one instance, the upward disturbance of 1950, did the variable actually move in a way consistent with balance-of-payments adjustment.

The fact that commercial bank borrowing from the central bank increased, as a rule, when the discount rate was raised and diminished when the rate was lowered may seem somewhat surprising. This relationship may be explained, however, in the light of concurrent changes in other variables. I will come back to this relationship after examining the other related variables.

[3] It should be recalled that data on discount rate variations are relevant, so far as the "basic" rate is concerned, only from August 1955 onward. Partial information on the manipulation of the "penalty rates" indicates, however, that discount rate variations were employed in an adjusting direction also during the downward disturbance of the first half of 1954 and the following upward disturbance of mid-1954 to the end of 1955.

The other component of the Bank of Japan's domestic claims is its net claims on the government. Unfortunately, the amount of such claims as they appear in the data is misleading, because the size of these claims is heavily affected, in a biased way, by foreign exchange movements. A decline in foreign exchange reserves, for instance, would usually, but not necessarily always, mean a (net) sale of foreign exchange (not drawn, most often, from the Bank) by the government's foreign exchange fund to the public. This, in turn, would increase the government's deposits at the Bank, or be used to redeem government debt to the Bank, thus reducing the government's net indebtedness to the Bank. An impression of a movement in an adjusting direction may thereby be created. But, in fact, the adjusting impact is that of the movement of foreign exchange itself, and recording its reflection in the government's accounts at the Bank would amount to double counting.[4]

In an indirect way, however, some conception of this variable can be gained by looking at the movements of the budgetary balance. As will be recalled, the government conducts its financial transactions (other than those in foreign exchange) primarily with the Bank of Japan rather than with the public or with commercial banks. Movements of the variable under consideration are, thus, primarily the mirror reflection of the government's cash balance. It will be observed later that this balance does not show a consistent reaction to imbalances of payments throughout the period and during the 1950's it may be regarded as having been changed most often in a disadjusting direction.

Due to the deficiency of the data on the Bank's net claims on the government, for the purpose at hand, the recorded magnitude of total domestic assets of the Bank may also be biased. However, it is not difficult, perhaps, to guess what an unbiased record would have shown. The budgetary balance, as has just been mentioned, usually did not tend to move in a way which would offset the movements of the Bank's claims on commercial banks: on the contrary, the two moved most often together, in a disadjusting direction. It may therefore be quite safely assumed that had bias-free data on the Bank's total domestic claims existed, they would have shown consistent movements in a disadjusting direction. Moreover, even without the necessary correction

4 From published sources, there does not seem to be a reliable way of separating the effect of the government's foreign exchange transactions from its other transactions.

(that is, including movements biased in an *adjusting* direction), the
data give the same indication. This is shown in column 4 of Table 1,
in which the frequency of movements in a disadjusting direction appears to be only slightly less than in column 3. This finding about the
direction of changes in the central bank's domestic assets is similar in
principle to those suggested by Nurkse and Bloomfield.[5]

Loans of commercial banks to the public are represented in column
5 of Table 1. They increased continuously at a rather fast pace
throughout the period under review, and the rate of increase appears
to be rather stable over the subperiods of balance-of-payments disturbances. The rate does not seem to vary much among these periods;
in the few instances where it does, the variations show no consistent
tendency either in the adjusting direction or in its opposite.

Money supply, on the other hand, which may be observed in column 6, does seem to react to balance-of-payments disturbances in an
adjusting direction, at least from the beginning of 1954. From that
period on, the rate of increase in money supply most of the time was
less during periods of downward disturbances in the balance of payments, and greater during periods of upward disturbances.

Turning to the fiscal variables, it appears much more difficult to
distinguish any consistent reaction to balance-of-payments disturbances. Both government revenues and expenditures show a clear long-
term expansionary trend, as should be expected. However, the rate of
increase, although not quite stable, does not seem to be associated
with balance-of-payments fluctuations.[6] The budgetary cash balance,
or the government's excess demand, is represented in column 7 of Table 1.[7] It appears that, for the period as a whole, no clear-cut pattern
may be distinguished. However, during the 1950's, movements of the
balance in a disadjusting direction do seem to dominate.

Let us now turn from the examination of subperiods of disturbances

[5] See, again, Nurkse, *International Currency Experience,* and Bloomfield, *Monetary Policy.*

[6] To save space, these variables are not shown in Table 1 and in Chart 1.

[7] Revenues and expenditures, and thus the budgetary balance, are compiled *net* of
the foreign exchange account of the budget. The latter, as has been pointed out
earlier, does not form a part of the government's excess demand; its inclusion would
not only have distorted the budgetary accounts for the purpose on hand but also
clearly introduced a bias in favor of movements in an adjusting direction.

From 1958 on, the budget is presented in this way in the source (*International
Financial Statistics*). For earlier years, the exclusion of revenues and expenditures in
the foreign exchange account was done by us.

TABLE 2

Japan: Reference Dates of Cycles
of Foreign Exchange Reserves

Cycle	Trough	Peak	Trough
1951–54	II 1951	III 1952	II 1954
1954–57	II 1954	IV 1956	III 1957
1957–61	III 1957	II 1961	IV 1961
1961–64	IV 1961	IV 1963	III 1964

to the application of reference cycle analysis.[8] In principle, the two methods should yield roughly the same indications, since they are rather similar: the cycle contains one subperiod of upward disturbance and one of downward disturbance—although it may also contain parts of subperiods of stability. However, using both methods may help to suggest patterns; and findings which are fully supported by both may deserve greater confidence. The cycle, in the present context, is that of foreign exchange reserves—which indeed manifest, as may be observed from Chart 1, rather clear cyclical movements. The reference dates will be determined by the turning points of these cycles, which will be defined from trough to trough. An expansionary phase (from trough to peak) will thus be the phase of the cycle in which foreign exchange reserves rise; and the contractionary phase—its opposite. The reference dates are shown in Table 2.

The positions of the policy variables during the reference-cycle stages are presented in Chart 2. In part A, it may be seen that the discount rate moves almost invariably in a consistent pattern—it falls when foreign exchange reserves rise (that is, along the stages from trough to peak), and rises when reserves fall. Bank of Japan claims on the public (i.e., on commercial banks), represented in part B, also follow a generally consistent pattern—falling during the expansionary phase of the cycle, and rising during the contraction. Total domestic assets of the Bank of Japan, shown in part C, reveal a weaker pattern:[9] during the expansionary phase, their level appears, as a rule,

[8] See, again, Burns and Mitchell, *Measuring Business Cycles*, Chapter 2.
[9] But, here, the distorting effect of the inclusion of foreign exchange transactions of the government should be recalled.

CHART 2

Japan: Patterns of Policy Variables
During Balance-of-Payments Cycles

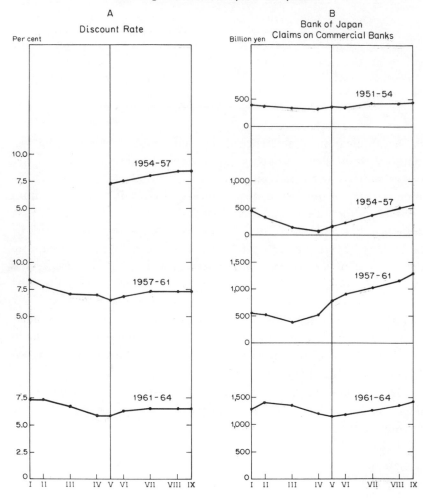

CHART 2 *(continued)*

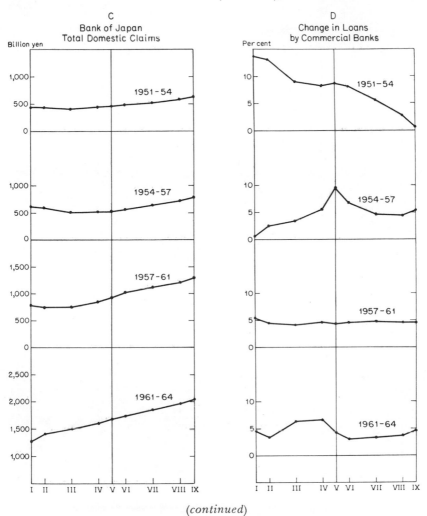

C
Bank of Japan
Total Domestic Claims

Billion yen

D
Change in Loans
by Commercial Banks

Per cent

1951–54

1954–57

1957–61

1961–64

(continued)

CHART 2 (*concluded*)

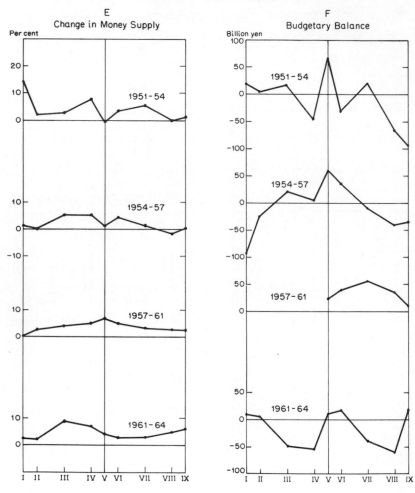

to be either falling or rising less fast than during the contractionary phase.

Commercial bank lending to the public, shown in part D, shows a probably slight dependence on the stage of the foreign exchange reserves cycle. Only during the cycle of II 1954–III 1957 does this manifest itself as clear-cut cyclical behavior, namely, an increase in the rate of expansion of credit when reserves rise, and a reduction of this rate when reserves fall. A similar but much weaker pattern appears also during the cycle of IV 1961–III 1964. It is thus apparent that this variable did occasionally respond in an adjusting direction, but that such response was far from being a general rule.

The rate of increase of money supply, drawn in part E, appears as a rule to be higher during the expansionary phase than during the subsequent contraction. This observation conforms, of course, to the tentative conclusion reached earlier. However, the pattern of behavior of this variable throughout each of these two phases is rather weak. Only once, in the 1957–61 cycle, does a neat, perfect pattern appear— of a gradual rise during the expansion, and a gradual decline during the contraction. In the 1954–57 cycle this pattern is approached, though not perfectly matched, while in the other two cycles, no such patterns can be found at all.

The positions of the budgetary balance, represented in part F, do not reveal any consistent pattern. No regular contrast appears, either with regard to the sign of the balance (surplus or deficit) or its form of movement between stages of rising and of falling foreign exchange reserves. This evidence tends to indicate that budgetary policy was not directed, as a rule, toward adjusting balance-of-payments disturbances.

Before trying to interpret these findings, we must ask whether the policy measures which were identified by this analysis as being taken to adjust balance-of-payments disturbances, may not in fact be related to other economic targets, movements of which happened to be associated in a consistent manner with balance-of-payments disturbances. We turn now to the examination of this possibility.

As will be recalled, alternative competing targets will be represented in the study by three variables: the rate of unemployment, the rate (and direction) of price changes, and the rate (and direction) of changes in industrial production. The unemployment rate, at least as it appears in available data, has been very low throughout the period under consideration. It is therefore assumed here, without further confirmation, that these changes could not, as a rule, have explained the policy measures taken. Even if this assumption is not fully warranted, it should be realized that the more significant changes in unemployment, at least, would not disappear from the analysis altogether, since these changes must be reflected in the rate of change of industrial production.

Two variables, standing for two targets, thus are left. One is the rate of change of the price level; the other, the rate of change in industrial production. Since the index of wholesale prices and the cost of living index (in Tokyo) give substantially the same indications of price movements, the latter index only will be used to represent this variable. The target of maintaining a stable price level will be considered violated here not when prices move, since prices moved upward almost continuously, but when their movement deviates from the price level's short-term trend (which is measured, in turn, by a three-year moving average).

The question posed is, thus, whether the manipulations of the discount rate and the budgetary balance could not be explained by either the wish to maintain a stable (movement of) price level or the wish to achieve a high rate of expansion of industrial production, rather than by the requirements of balance-of-payments adjustment. Again, more than one method will be used to test this hypothesis.

Take first the discount rate. In Table 3, each change in this variable is shown for the period from 1957 onward (the change in early 1957 being the first since August 1955 when the "basic" discount rate became meaningful). The direction of change of each of the three alternative target variables—foreign exchange reserves, the price level, and industrial production—is examined in each quarter in which the discount rate moved. If the direction of the latter movement is consistent with the assumption that it was made in order to adjust a certain target variable, in view of the concurrent change in that variable, the latter is given a plus sign for that quarter; if the change in the discount rate is in the opposite direction, the variable is assigned a minus. It is thus possible to get an impression at a glance of whether an assumption that manipulation of the discount rate was intended to serve a certain target is justified or, rather, not contradicted, by the data.

` TABLE 3

Japan: Changes in the Discount Rate and Movements of Policy Targets

Quarter	Discount Rate (1)	Foreign Exchange Reserves (2)	Price Level (Cost of Living Index) Compared with Trend (3)	Industrial Production (rate of change) (4)
I 1957	raised	+ fall	* stable	+ increases
II 1957	raised	+ fall	+ rises	+ increases
II 1958	lowered	+ rise	− rises	+ declines
III 1958	lowered	+ rise	+ falls	* stable
I 1959	lowered	+ rise	+ falls	− increases
IV 1959	raised	− rise	+ rises	+ increases
III 1960	lowered	+ rise	− rises	* stable
I 1961	lowered	+ rise	− rises	− increases
III 1961	raised	+ fall	+ rises	+ increases
IV 1962	lowered	+ rise	* stable	+ declines
I 1963	lowered	+ rise	− rises	* stable
II 1963	lowered	+ rise	− rises	− increases
I 1964	raised	+ fall	− falls	+ increases
I 1965	lowered	+ rise	− rises	+ declines
II 1965	lowered	− fall	− rises	+ declines

Note: + The change in the target variable would justify the direction of change in the discount rate.
      − The change in the target variable would justify the opposite direction.
      * The change in the target variable would call for no change in the discount rate.

It appears immediately that the movements of the discount rate are consistent with the assumption that this instrument was used for balance-of-payments adjustment—not a surprising finding, of course, at this stage of the analysis since a similar finding was the starting point of the present test. Table 3 also shows, however, that changes in the discount rate are not, as a rule, compatible with the assumption that they were intended to maintain a stable rate of change in the price level. This assumption is, indeed, so obviously contradicted by the data that it will not be subject here to further investigation. No such clear-cut indication is provided about the rate of expansion of industrial production. The assumption that discount rate policy was motivated by a desire to maintain stability on a high level in this rate ap-

pears to be refuted on a number of occasions, but not often enough
to be dismissed on this evidence.

Additional evidence is provided, however, in Table 4 and Chart 3.
In Table 4, subperiods of balance-of-payments disturbances serve
again as units of observation. It may be seen immediately that the
movements of the discount rate in each of these subperiods—with not
a single exception—could be explained by a wish to correct imbalances
of payments, but not by the desire to maintain a high rate of expansion in production. In the reference cycle analysis shown in Chart 3,
the reference dates are determined by cycles in the rate of change of
industrial production. The trough is defined as the point at which this
rate is lowest (in rare cases it is even negative), and the peak as where

TABLE 4

Japan: The Discount Rate and Industrial Production
During Subperiods of Disturbances

Subperiod	Foreign Exchange Reserves (1)	Industrial Production (rate of change) (2)	Discount Rate (3)
II–IV 1950	rise	n.a.	a
IV 1950–II 1951	fall	n.a.	a
II 1951–III 1952	rise	declines slightly	a
III 1952–II 1953	fall	stable	a
II–IV 1953	stable	increases slightly	a
IV 1953–II 1954	fall	declines slightly	a
II 1954–IV 1955	rise	stable	a
IV 1955–IV 1956	stable	increases	+ stable
IV 1956–III 1957	fall	no trend	+ raised
III 1957–II 1961	rise	no trend	+ reduced considerably
II–IV 1961	fall	stable	+ raised
IV 1961–II 1963	rise	declines and then increases	+ reduced considerably
II–IV 1963	stable	increases	+ stable
IV 1963–II 1964	fall	stable	+ raised

Note: + The policy variable changes in the direction required for balance-of-payments adjustment; no change would be justified by the movement of industrial production.
a not applicable.

CHART 3

Japan: Pattern of the Discount Rate
During Industrial Production Cycles

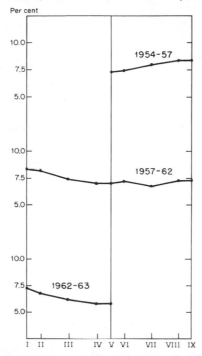

it is highest. It appears that a largely consistent pattern is displayed: in the trough, the discount rate is high; it is lowered towards the peak, when the rate is lowest, and raised again during the movement from peak to trough. However, this, of course, is the exact opposite of what a policy intended to lead to a high rate of expansion would have required. The actual policy followed reduced the discount rate—an expansionary measure—when the rate of expansion of production was highest, and raised the discount rate when expansion slowed down, that is, exactly when a fall of the discount rate would have been called for.[10] This evidence seems to provide another strong basis for

[10] The inverse relationship between the discount rate and the expansion of industrial production could, on the other hand, be explained by the opposite causal connection; namely, high interest rates lead to contractions, and low rates to expansions. An examination of the validity of such a statement, in general or in the specific case of Japan, is clearly beyond the scope of the present study.

rejecting the assumption that discount rate policy was intended to promote a high rate of growth. The assumption, on the other hand, that this policy was manipulated in the interests of balance-of-payments adjustment is strongly supported by these tests.

Table 5 describes the two alternative target variables—foreign exchange reserves and industrial production—during periods in which the budget displayed clearly either surpluses or deficits. It may be seen,

TABLE 5

Japan: The Budgetary Balance and Movements of Policy Targets

Period	Budgetary Balance (1)	Foreign Exchange Reserves (2)	Industrial Production (rate of increase) (3)
IV 1950–II 1951	surplus	* stable	n.a.
IV 1953–I 1955	deficit	* no trend	+ low
II 1955–I 1957	surplus	− rise	+ high
II 1960–IV 1961	surplus	* no trend	* normal
III 1962–III 1963	deficit	+ rise	+ low

Note: See Table 3 for explanation of symbols.

from column 2, that the assumption that budgetary policy was used to adjust balance-of-payments disturbances could not be sustained by this evidence: it is supported by only a single episode—that of the budgetary deficit of III 1962–III 1963—out of the five listed in Table 5. The alternative assumption, that budgetary policy was used to serve the target of a high rate of expansion of industrial production, fares much better: it is supported by three episodes (out of four), and clearly rejected by none.

3. Summary and Interpretation

From all the evidence presented, it appears that budgetary policy in Japan did not usually serve as an instrument for adjusting balance-of-payments disequilibria. It seems possible that, insofar as budgetary policy was regarded as a tool to be used in the pursuance of economic policy, it was allocated to the target of preserving a high rate of expansion of economic activity.

Monetary developments, on the other hand, definitely appear to respond to the movements of the balance of payments, and monetary policy may be viewed as being geared to the needs of balance-of-payments adjustment. Imbalances of payments lead to changes in monetary variables in accordance with the following typical pattern.

In a downward disturbance, that is, a downward tendency of foreign exchange reserves, the Bank of Japan invariably reacts by raising the discount rate. From the information available, it also seems likely that the Bank would use "moral suasion," or "discount-window guidance," in an effort to restrict the amount of credit extended by commercial banks to their customers. At the same time, however, the change in the public's *demand* for this credit would be expected to move in the opposite direction. This is a period in which the amount of liquidity available to the economy from the (net) acquisition of foreign exchange reserves is falling, that is, the loss of reserves tends to diminish the amount of liquid means. As a result, demand for bank credit by the public must rise. In the end, the rate of credit expansion may tend to show a slight tendency to fall during downward disturbances, although this tendency is far from being consistent. This seems to be an indication that the aforementioned restrictions on the supply of credit are effective. To what extent this may be attributed to cost restrictions (through the increase of the discount rate), or how much of it may be due to direct quantitative restrictions ("window guidance"), is impossible to tell on the basis of available information.[11]

But even when the rate of credit expansion does fall, this tendency

[11] The increase in the discount rate would act as a cost restriction in either of two ways. If the rates charged by banks on loans to their customers remain unchanged, the increased cost incurred by the banks themselves on their borrowing from the central bank would act as a deterrent to their borrowing and relending (or lending and rediscounting). If, on the other hand, the banks "pass on" the increase in their cost by raising the interest rates charged on their lending, the amount of credit demanded by the public should tend to decline. As a rule, the former channel was probably more important in the Japanese case. The rates charged by banks were subject to legal ceilings; usually, the rates found in effect were the ceiling rates. Thus, changes in the discount rate were not transformed into changes in the various rates charged by the banks, but acted through the reduction of profitability of the banks' lending. This, in turn, should presumably lead the banks, in such a time, to increase the proportion of favored, less risky loans in their total lending. The special difficulties realized in fact by Japan's small business sector during such periods may be an indication that this indeed was the process.

is only slight. To maintain the expansion of credit, commercial banks must take some compensatory action with regard to their own liquidity or reserves. Bank liquidity is affected by three major factors (disregarding the possibility of changes in the public's desired currency ratio): changes in the amount of foreign exchange reserves, changes in the amount of central bank lending to the government, and changes in central bank lending to the commercial banks themselves. Information about the second factor is deficient; but it does not seem likely that it operates with enough force to even nearly offset the operation of the first factor, namely, changes in foreign exchange reserves. Thus, in order to resist the downward pressure on their liquidity the banks resort to increased borrowing from the central bank. They do so despite the increased cost of this borrowing—presumably, as has been explained, as a result of increased demand by the public for bank credit.[12]

Money supply, in its turn, is affected by three major factors (disregarding the possibility of a change in the proportion of liquid assets held by the public in the form of assets not defined as money, such as time deposits). These are the changes in foreign exchange reserves, in central bank (net) lending to the government, and in the amount of bank lending (in all forms) to the public. A downward disturbance, as defined here, consists of a fall in foreign exchange reserves. Central bank lending to the government may, at most, only partly offset this movement; whereas the third component—bank lending to the public —tends somewhat to reinforce it. The net result is that, when foreign exchange reserves fall, the amount of money (more precisely, in the case of Japan, the rate of expansion of this amount) tends to fall too.

In a period of an upward disturbance, this pattern is reversed; and Bank of Japan lending to the government most often tends to increase. Commercial banks use the added liquidity acquired by them

[12] The tendency of commercial banks to increase their borrowing from the central bank when they suffer a loss of liquidity due to a decline of foreign exchange reserves, and, conversely, to repay debts to the central bank when additional liquidity is acquired through the rise of foreign exchange reserves, was recognized and emphasized in Nurkse's classic study, *International Currency Experience*, especially p. 70. Nurkse offered this tendency, which he termed "automatic neutralization," as a partial explanation of his finding that the "rules of the game" were not observed during the interwar period. Bloomfield (*Monetary Policy Under the International Gold Standard*, pp. 50–51) used it in a similar way in his analysis of the pre-1914 gold standard. But see the discussion of this topic in Chapter 2 of the present study.

not to increase the rate of expansion of their lending to the public but to repay debts to the Bank of Japan—despite the fall in the latter's discount rate, which is a practically invariable consequence in this situation. The rate of expansion of bank credit remains stable, or tends to rise, and the rate of expansion of money supply accelerates.

To sum up: the discount rate and the rate of expansion of money supply respond consistently to imbalance of payments. At times of downward disturbances, the discount rate is raised, and the money supply falls, whereas the opposite tendencies are manifested in episodes of upward disturbances. These, of course, are tendencies consistent with the assumption that monetary policy was used to adjust the balance of payments.

4

GERMANY

1. Policy Instruments

MONETARY POLICY

Monetary policy in Germany is conducted by the Deutsche Bundesbank, which was established by the Bank Act of July 1957. The Bundesbank is headed by a Central Bank Council, which consists of the president, the vice president, and the presidents of the Central Banks in the states (Länder). All of these are appointed by the President of the Federal Republic. The *Länder* Central Banks are, in fact, branches of the Bundesbank. Before 1957, central banking in Germany was conducted by the Bank Deutscher Länder [BDL], which was established in November 1948. This bank differed somewhat in concept from its successor by having a more decentralized structure. It was conceived as the coordinating body of the Länder Central Banks, and its president was elected by their directors. However, the differences in mode of operation between the Bundesbank and its predecessor, the BDL, were of minor significance.

The Bundesbank is autonomous, and is not subject to any direction by the federal government. The 1957 Bank Act provides for participation of government representatives—without voting rights—in meetings of the Bundesbank Council, and of the Bundesbank president in the government's deliberations on monetary policy. But the Bundesbank is not bound in any way by the government, nor is it committed to fulfill any government request or requirement. The Bundesbank does, of course, act as the government's banking agent. The federal government and the *Länder* are committed to hold their deposits at the Bundesbank. They may hold deposits at other banks only with the Bundesbank's consent. Under this provision the latter has granted the Länder governments rights to hold deposits, within specified

quotas, at certain financial institutions. The Bundesbank is entitled
to grant the federal government, the *Länder,* and certain public Special Funds short-term credits within quotas specified in the Bank Act.
This does not mean, however, that the Bundesbank is committed to
extend these credits. Decisions on credits within the quotas are made
at the Bundesbank's discretion.

The Bundesbank has at its disposal all of the major conventional
tools of monetary policy and has used them extensively. These instruments will be surveyed here briefly.

Discount Rate. The Bank buys and sells short-term bills (up to three
months) which fulfill certain requirements at the fixed discount rate.
These include, among others, Treasury bills and bills issued by the
Länder or other public authorities. The discount rate has in fact been
uniform, at any given point of time, for all the bills; but the Bank, in
principle, has the right to discriminate among various categories of
bills.

The Bank also makes loans to commercial banks against collateral.
The securities eligible for collateral are government bills and bonds
or other debentures listed by the Bank. The interest rate applied to
such loans is usually 1 per cent above the discount rate. Lending in
this form is not automatic; it is presumably intended to meet short-
term liquidity gaps at the commercial banks. The interest rate charged
by banks on loans to their customers is tied by law to the discount
rate, which it cannot exceed by more than a specified percentage. As
long as the difference between the two rates is this maximum, any
reduction of the discount rate leads directly to an equivalent reduction in the interest rate charged by banks on their lending (although
this would not necessarily hold true for an increase). Often, however,
the gap between the two rates is less than the specified maximum, so
that the effect of discount rate changes on rates charged by the banks
is not automatic and is less direct.

The Bank is entitled, and has consistently used its right, to specify
a maximum rediscount quota for each individual bank. This quota is
usually determined on the basis of the bank's capital: it is a certain
coefficient of the size of the capital, but the coefficient may vary among
classes of banks. The Bank has used changes in this coefficient, and

thus in the individual quotas, as an instrument of monetary policy on a number of occasions.

Open-Market Operations. The Bundesbank is entitled to buy and sell all the bills eligible for rediscounting at the Bank, as well as other bills or bonds issued by the federal government, the *Länder,* and other public authorities, and also private bonds quoted on the stock exchange.

In fact, open-market operations were of minor significance in the earlier years, since the central bank (at that time, the BDL) had had almost no portfolio of marketable securities. By mid-1955, however, the central bank reached an agreement with the government, which in 1957 was incorporated in the Bank Act, putting a substantial amount of such securities at the Bank's disposal. This was done by transforming the character of the "equalization claims," i.e., the Bank's claims on the government resulting from the Bank's assumption of the government's obligations towards the commercial banks, which in turn were a product of the currency reform of 1948. Originally, these claims carried an interest rate of 3 per cent, and could be sold only at their nominal value; in fact, this provision meant that the claims were not marketable. The agreement under consideration freed the Bank to sell (and buy) these claims at other prices. The claims, which subsequently became known also as the "Mobilization Paper," originally amounted to some eight billion marks. Open-market operations, which since 1956 have assumed large proportions, have been conducted primarily in this paper.

An agreement between the Bank and the commercial banks leads, in fact, to excluding the nonbank private sector from participation in the market for the paper in which the Bank's open-market transactions are conducted; that is, open-market operations are made only between the Bank and commercial banks, without any *immediate* effect on the nonbank sector.

An important attribute of open-market operations in Germany is that the Bundesbank directly determines not quantity but *price* in these transactions. The Bank specifies an interest rate—that is, by implication, prices of securities—at which the Bank is willing to buy or sell eligible securities offered to it or demanded from it. The interest rate varies, as a rule, with the length of maturity of the security (Mobilization Paper has been issued with various maturities). This, of course, is a procedure quite similar to determining the Bank's discount rate. Indeed, the open-market rate has, as a rule, been quite close to the discount rate; but variations in the open-market posted rate have been much more frequent than in the discount rate.

Reserve Requirements. Minimum reserve requirements have been in effect since 1948, and are incorporated in the Bank Act of 1957. The Bundesbank is entitled to require that the commercial banks hold reserves in the form of current balances at the Bundesbank. The requirements may vary among classes of banks and according to the type of liability against which reserves are held. The maximum ratios provided for in the act were 30 per cent for sight deposits, 20 per cent for time deposits and 10 per cent for savings deposits. In addition to the distinction as to the type of liabilities, the Bundesbank requirements distinguish between banks in "bank places"—that is, places in which branches of the Bundesbank are located—and other banks; the former are subject to higher reserve requirements. Likewise, banks are divided into six categories according to the size of their liabilities; the larger the bank, the higher the reserve requirements. The number of different reserve-ratio requirements existing at any moment of time is, thus, quite substantial (approximately fifteen to twenty). As a rule, this structure moves in a coordinated way, and the proportional differences among the various ratios remain about constant.

Most of the time, reserve requirements were put on an average (or total) basis for each class of bank and liability. During a short period, however, *marginal* reserve ratios were added. In July 1960, all increases in liabilities above their average level of March–May 1960 were subject to the maximum reserve requirements, while liabilities of the average size of March–May 1960 were subject to lower requirements. This situation lasted until December 1960, when the marginal reserve requirements were withdrawn.

Shortages of reserves are subject to penalty rates of 3 per cent above the rate in force for the Bank's advances against collateral. This means, as a rule, an interest rate 4 per cent over the discount rate.

Changes in reserve requirements were made about as often as they were in the discount rate; they were, thus, much less frequent than variations in the Bank's open-market rates. It seems that the Bundesbank regarded open-market operations as the main instrument for effecting gradual changes in bank liquidity and in interest rates; while changes in the discount rate and in reserve ratio requirements were made at longer intervals as a means of consolidating and reinforcing the effect of open-market operations.

Reserve requirements were used by the Bundesbank on a few occasions to directly influence commercial banks' policy towards holding assets or borrowing abroad. This was done by subjecting foreign deposits in German banks, and the latter's borrowings from abroad, to special reserve requirements and by varying these requirements. Likewise, German banks' holdings abroad were regarded as a reserve asset held against liabilities to foreigners on a number of occasions when the Bundesbank considered short-term investments of German banks abroad to be desirable.

FISCAL POLICY

For most purposes of analyzing fiscal policy in Germany, the category "government" should include the *Länder* as well as the federal government. The reason is that the budgets of these two bodies are quite closely integrated, particularly on the revenue side. The German Constitution specifies the allocation of the various tax revenues. In some cases (such as the business tax), all tax proceeds belong to the *Länder*. In others, they belong to the federal government. The proceeds of the income tax are divided between the two—about two-thirds to the *Länder* and one-third to the federal government. In addition, revenues are reallocated among the *Länder*—those with higher tax proceeds transfer part of their revenues to the others. Likewise, most of the tax laws of each *Land* have to be approved by the appropriate federal bodies. All of this would indicate the need to add the *Länder* to the federal government in discussions of budgets and budgetary policy.

In the federal government, budgetary policy is left in the hands of the executive branch to a probably greater extent than in most other Western countries. The Cabinet (and within it the Chancellor and the Minister of Finance) has a veto power over budgetary decisions. The executive branch's leeway is particularly large in "negative" acts; that is, the Cabinet is quite free not to make certain expenditures, or not to raise revenue from certain taxes, even though it is entitled to do so by the budgetary law of that year.

The federal budget is divided into "ordinary" (above the line) and "extraordinary" (below the line) components. In principle, "ordinary" budget expenditures should be covered by tax revenues, while expenditures of the "extraordinary" budget could be covered by loans as long as they result in the acquisition of "self-liquidating" assets. In fact, this requirement is interpreted in a way which puts very few restrictions on the type of expenditures in the latter budget. Yet, the declared policy of the German government has been to maintain a (cash) balance in the over-all budget; and this indeed has been the policy over long stretches of time.

2. Statistical Analysis

The analysis of policy reactions to balance-of-payments disturbances seems particularly complicated in Germany due to the largely one-sided nature of the imbalances. During the years 1952–58, that is, for about half of the total period covered, there was a continual surplus in the balance of payments, and foreign exchange reserves kept accumulating. This makes it impossible to examine policy reactions to changes in the balance of payments from deficits to surpluses, and vice versa, during these years. To overcome this difficulty—to some extent, at least—several approaches may be explored.

First, one might analyze just the years remaining after the 1952–58 period is subtracted, in which periodic changes in the direction of the imbalance did occur. Two periods of downward movement can be distinguished prior to the continuous upward movement of reserves which started in 1952; they took place in late 1950 to early 1951, and a year later. These can certainly be viewed as periods of disturbances. Upward movements of reserves during most of 1950 and most of 1951, on the other hand, may not have been regarded as disturbances. They may have been part of the general strong upward trend of reserves which lasted until the end of 1958; that is, the German government may have considered these upward movements desirable, rather than as indicative of disturbances. From 1959 on, each downward or upward movement could be considered a disturbance; a slight over-all rising trend in reserves is still found in these years but the trend factor is not large in comparison to the size of the periodical fluctuations. The subperiods are determined by both the series of foreign exchange reserves and, since 1958, of balance-of-payments surpluses or deficits. By and large, the two series give the same indications for the years covered by both. Sometimes, the two may differ by one quarter in their indication of the turning point. In the very few cases of clear conflict between the two series, the turning point was selected by reference to the series of balance-of-payments surpluses and deficits.

Table 6 shows subperiods of disturbances. The table covers two periods of downward disturbances prior to 1952, and all the post-1958 period—the latter containing three subperiods of downward and two subperiods of upward disturbances. Altogether, seven subperiods of imbalances are represented in Table 6. This is not a large number of observations, yet it provides quite a strong impression of the policy behavior pattern—at least in the negative sense.

A look, first, at the discount rate (column 2) shows clearly that this instrument has not been used generally for balance-of-payments adjustment. In only two downward disturbances, the one following the outbreak of the Korean war and the one which started in mid-1964, was the discount rate manipulated in the direction that balance-of-payments adjustment would require. During the other disturbances, the discount rate was either kept stable or moved in both directions within each subperiod of imbalance.

The posted rate for open-market operations (column 3) shows much the same behavior. Again, in one recent imbalance only—the downward movement of mid-1964 to early 1966—was this rate changed in the direction required for balance-of-payments adjustment. Thus, open-market operations do not appear to have been intended to serve generally the target of balance-of-payments equilibrium.

The same impression is conveyed by the fluctuations of reserve ratio requirements, which are shown in column 4. Once more, only during the 1950–51 and the 1964 and subsequent disequilibria did reserve ratio requirements move in the direction necessary for adjustment.

It thus appears that all the three major direct instruments at the disposal of the German central bank—changes of the discount rate, open-market operations, and changes of minimum reserve ratio requirements—have not been used, as a rule, for balance-of-payments

TABLE 6

Germany: Movements of Policy Variables
During Subperiods of Disturbances

Subperiod	Gold and Foreign Exchange Reserves (indication of disturbance) (1)	Discount Rate (2)	Open-Market Rate (3)	Reserve Ratio Requirements (4)	Central Bank Claims on Commercial Banks (5)
III 1950–I 1951	fall	+ raised	a	+ raised	− rise
III 1951–I 1952	fall	* stable	a	* stable	* no trend
IV 1958–III 1959	fall	* no trend	* no trend	* stable	* stable
III 1959–II 1961	rise	* no trend	* no trend	− raised	* no trend
II 1961–I 1962	fall	* stable	− reduced	− reduced	* stable
I 1962–I 1963	stable	stable	raised	stable	rise
I 1963–II 1964	rise	* stable	* stable	* stable	+ rise
II 1964–	fall	+ raised	+ raised	+ raised	− rise

Subperiod	Central Bank Net Claims on Government (6)	Central Bank Total Domestic Claims (7)	Commercial Bank Lending to Public (rate of change) (8)	Money Supply (rate of change) (9)	Budgetary Balance (10)
III 1950–I 1951	* stable	− rise	+ falls	+ falls	n.a.
III 1951–I 1952	+ fall	+ fall	* stable	* stable	balanced
IV 1958–III 1959	− rise	− rise	n.a.	+ falls	− large deficit
III 1959–II 1961	− fall	− fall	n.a.	− falls	no trend
II 1961–I 1962	− rise	− rise	+ falls	− rises	− small deficit
I 1962–I 1963	no trend	rise	stable	falls	small deficit
I 1963–II 1964	* no trend	+ rise	* stable	* stable	+ deficit
II 1964–	− rise	− rise sharply	* stable	* stable	* deficit

Note: + indicates a movement in the direction required for balance-of-payment
        adjustment.
      − indicates a movement in the opposite direction.
      * indicates no movement or a very slight one.
  n.a. = not available.
  a not applicable.

adjustment. There are only two instances which *may* be exceptions, i.e., the downward disturbances of late 1950 and early 1951 and of mid-1964 to early 1966.

Looking at the policy variables which involve the central bank's assets, similar indications appear, perhaps even more strongly. Central bank lending to the commercial banking system (represented in column 5 of Table 6) appears to be unrelated to balance-of-payments fluctuations. Central bank net lending to the government (in column 6) seems to move less often in the direction required for balance-of-payments adjustment than in the opposite direction; this is particularly true for the post-1958 period. Changes in this category are mainly due, in the case of Germany, not to changes in the central bank's gross lending to the government but to changes in the amount of government deposits at the central bank. As may be seen by comparing column 6 with column 10 (or the appropriate lines in Chart 4), fluctuations in the central bank's net lending to the government are to some extent related to the government's budgetary surpluses and deficits. But the correlation is not perfect due to the reflection of two other factors aside from the budgetary balance in the size of the government's net indebtedness to the Bank; namely, open-market operations and the distribution of government deposits between the Bank and other banks.

Since the Bank's lending to commercial banks does not move in conformity with the requirements of balance-of-payments adjustment, while net lending to the government moves most often in the direction opposite to these requirements, the Bank's total domestic assets—the combination of these two—most of the time moves counter to the requirements of balance-of-payments adjustment. This is shown in column 7 of Table 6. According to the Nurkse-Bloomfield yardstick, Germany is thus seen to follow a pattern of monetary policy, during the subperiods under observation, opposite to what the classical "rules of the game" would require.

Commercial bank lending (shown in column 8) does not seem to vary in any consistent way with imbalances of payments. In only one instance—the downward disturbance of II 1961–I 1962—did the rate of credit expansion change in conformity with the requirements for balance-of-payments adjustment: it was considerably below the rate in the preceding and succeeding periods, in which foreign exchange re-

CHART 4

Germany: Time Series of Selected Variables

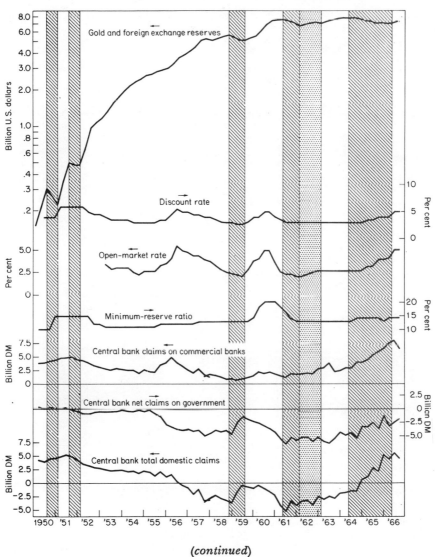

(continued)

CHART 4 (concluded)

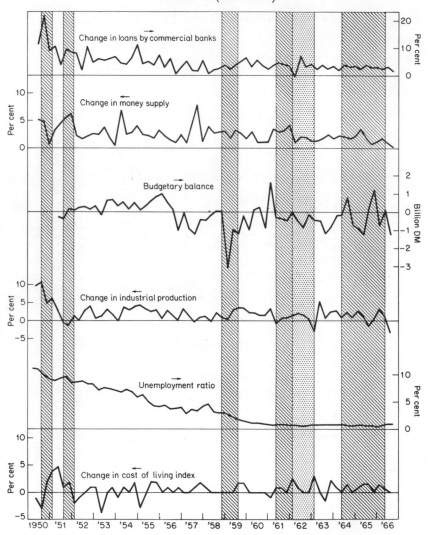

Note: Diagonal-line areas represent periods of downward imbalances; gray areas represent stability; and white areas represent upward imbalances.

serves increased. In other instances, the rate of credit expansion remained usually rather stable. Thus it may be deduced that the amount
of credit (or, more precisely, its rate of expansion) was not manipulated in accordance with the requirements for balance-of-payments adjustment, although it cannot be said that an opposite pattern emerges
either. The rate of expansion of money supply (represented in column
9) gives a similar indication. This rate is quite stable most of the
time, and the modest changes in it move as often in the adjusting direction as in the opposite. Thus, although it cannot be argued that
money supply changed consistently in a disadjusting direction, it
seems fairly obvious that this variable did not move, in any general
way, in the direction required for balance-of-payments adjustment. By
this yardstick too, monetary policy in Germany did not conform to the
classical "rules of the game."

Turning finally to the fiscal area, the conclusions are similar. As
may be seen from column 10 of Table 6, the budgetary (cash) balance did not fluctuate in any consistent way with imbalances of payments. Moreover, it should be added that the balances (surpluses or
deficits) were in general too small, in comparison with components
such as the GNP, changes in foreign exchange reserves, etc., to be expected to have any appreciable effect on the economy. It is thus most
probable that budgetary balances were not manipulated at all as a
means of achieving either balance-of-payments adjustments or any of
the other major economic targets.

We now turn to the period of continually rising foreign exchange
reserves, from early 1952 to the end of 1958. Let us examine a few criti-
cal policy variables for this period to see whether their behavior is
consistent with the assumption that they were manipulated in accordance with the requirements of balance-of-payments adjustment. These
variables are: (1) The direct monetary instruments—the discount rate,
the open-market rate, and the minimum-reserve ratios; (2) the rate of
expansion of money supply; (3) the budgetary balance.

To assist in balance-of-payments adjustment, the discount rate, the
open-market rate, and the minimum-reserve ratio would have to move
downward during a period of accumulating reserves. Such a movement did not, in fact, take place—or if it did, was only slight—as may
be seen from Chart 4. The discount rate went down from 1952 to 1954,
up from 1955 to mid-1956, and down again until mid-1959. The over-

all trend of the rate was indeed downward, but it appears insignificant in comparison with the extensive movements of the rate within these years. Moreover, to the degree this trend existed, it went on during later years and thus cannot be assumed to be a response to accumulating reserves. The open-market rate is a relevant variable, it will be recalled, only after mid-1955. Starting then, it went up until mid-1956 and thereafter moved downward until mid-1959—in close relationship to the movements of the discount rate. The required reserve ratio was much more stable than the former two rates. It went slightly down in 1952–53, and up in 1955–57; over-all, it can probably be regarded as having been stable during the years under review. By this evidence, therefore, these three monetary variables are found to have played a neutral role, on the average, with regard to balance-of-payments adjustment: they were manipulated neither in the direction required for adjustment nor in the opposite direction.

The rate of expansion in the money supply conveys a similar impression. This rate was, on the average, much lower during 1952–58 than during 1950–51 and only slightly higher than during 1959–65. On the other hand, balance-of-payments adjustment policy would have required this rate to be particularly high during 1952–58. Taking into account the fact that the GNP's rate of increase has shown a downward trend, a fact which may account for a desire on the part of the monetary authority to gradually slow down the expansion of money supply, it cannot be argued that money supply was manipulated in a way which would contradict the need for balance-of-payment adjustment. However, the evidence certainly would not support the opposite assumption, i.e., that the supply moved in a way which would be consistent with the requirements for balance-of-payments adjustment during 1952–58.

The budgetary balance, as may again be seen from Chart 4, gives a similar indication. From 1952 to mid-1956, the budget had a consistent surplus—in fact, only in a single quarter (II 1953) was this not the case. From mid-1956 to the end of 1958, the budget had mostly deficits. For the period under review as a whole, the budgetary balance was positive, while for the following years—1959–65—the budget had deficits during most of the time and a net deficit for those years as a whole. The substantial budgetary surplus for 1952–55—at least for most of the period—is alleged to have arisen accidentally.[1] It may well be so, but this would still not contradict the conclusion that during a period in which balance-of-payments adjustment would have required a budgetary deficit, the budget showed, in fact, mostly a surplus. It may thus be inferred that budgetary policy during the period 1952–58 was not employed as an instrument of balance-of-payments adjustment.

Thus, during 1952–58 neither monetary policy nor budgetary policy seem to have been manipulated in a way consistent with balance-of-payments requirements. This conclusion is similar to the one reached before in reference to earlier periods of imbalances, as well as to the later years 1959–65. The over-all finding which emerges is that monetary instruments and the budget were, by and large, not employed in Germany for balance-of-payments adjustment during the period covered in the present study.

Were these instruments used, instead, to achieve alternative targets? An attempt to analyze this question will be made with the aid of the reference cycle method. Here, the "cycle" is determined by fluctuations of the *policy variable;* and movements of each target variable are examined separately to see whether any of them could explain the cyclical pattern of the policy variable. This will not be done for the budgetary variable; as was mentioned before, the size of the budgetary balance—surplus or deficit—appears to be rather small most of the time, and it is apparently not meaningful to discuss "cycles" of this variable. The reference cycle analysis will be confined, thus, to the direct monetary instruments: the discount rate, the open-market rate, and the minimum-reserve ratio. These show a clear "cyclical" pattern, and the question analyzed is whether this pattern can be associated with the movement of any target variable. The reference dates will therefore be determined by the turning points of these policy variables. As was mentioned before, and as may be verified again by observing

---

[1] This is the famous "Juliustrum," or the "Julius Tower" war chest. It resulted, allegedly, from the accumulation during the early 1950's of funds intended to finance Germany's participation in the planned European Defense Community—a plan which was eventually scrapped. It is hard to believe that the German authorities indeed based their policy on a rule which says that surpluses should be created during certain years in order to finance deficits in later years, without regard to the effects of the surpluses and deficits at the time in which they are maintained. It is possible, on the other hand, that in each of these individual years actual military expenditures were lower than had been anticipated and provided for in the budget, thus leading to a surplus.

Chart 4, these three rates fluctuated in close coordination; very rarely did they move in opposing directions. This makes it possible to define a combined reference cycle for all three instruments. The turning points, or reference dates, will be determined, whenever just one variable moves while the others are stable, by that variable which moved. The trough of such a cycle will be at the point in which the discount rate, the open-market rate, and the minimum-reserve ratio are at their lowest; while the peak will occur when they are at their highest. The results are shown in Chart 5, where the behavior of each of the alternative target variables—the balance of payments, the price level, the unemployment rate, and the rate of expansion in industrial production—is shown along the reference cycles. The turning points of these cycles are as follows:

Period	Trough	Peak	Trough
1950–54	IV 1950	I 1952	III 1954
1954–59	III 1954	II 1956	II 1959
1959–62	II 1959	III 1960	I 1962
1962–66	I 1962	III 1966	

Chart 5, part A, shows the movement of foreign exchange reserves. As could be expected from the previous analysis, no regularity can be seen here. Conformity with balance-of-payments adjustment would require this variable to fall during the trough-to-peak phase—that is, where the discount rate and the other rates are rising—and to rise during the peak-to-trough phase. In fact, nothing resembling such a pattern can be discerned.

It may be worthwhile to examine alternative definitions of the balance-of-payments target in order to see whether they can give a better clue to policy measures than the simple change in foreign exchange reserves (that is, the simple balance-of-payments surplus or deficit as these are usually defined). Thus, it is conceivable that monetary measures were taken in reaction not to changes in the balance-of-payments as a whole, but to movements in the trade account alone. This is examined in Chart 5, part B, where the balance of trade (in goods) is represented. Again, no regular pattern appears. This balance was continuously positive after about mid-1952. An assumption that movements of this variable determined the direction of movement of the policy variables would require the balance to have been negative along the

CHART 5

Germany: Patterns of Target Variables
During Monetary Policy Cycles

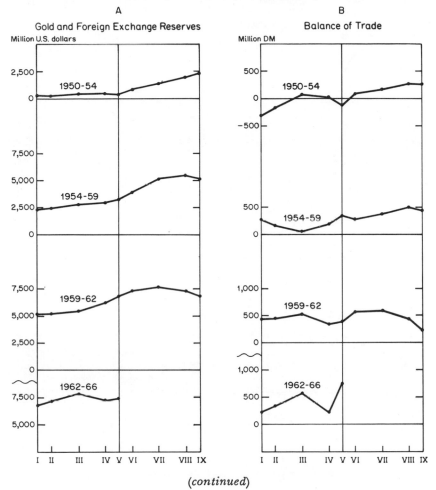

A
Gold and Foreign Exchange Reserves

B
Balance of Trade

(continued)

CHART 5 (*continued*)

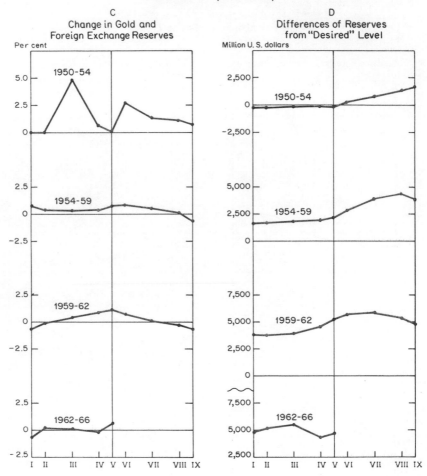

CHART 5 (*continued*)

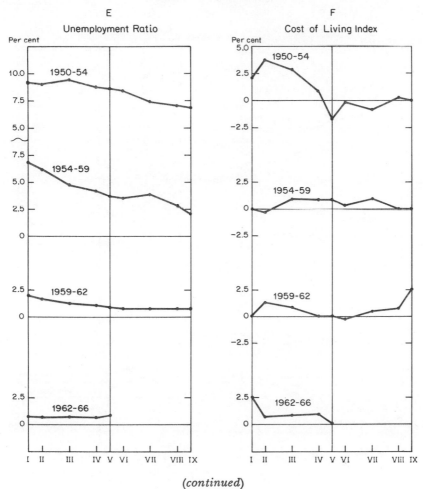

E
Unemployment Ratio

F
Cost of Living Index

(*continued*)

CHART 5 *(concluded)*

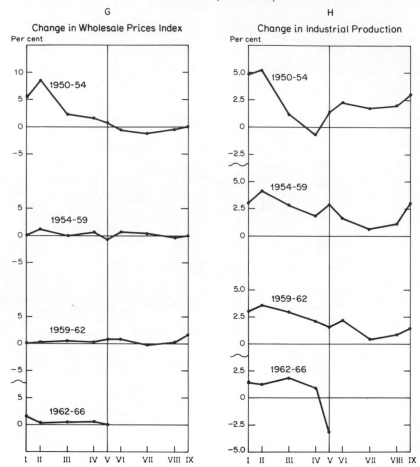

trough-to-peak phase, or at least to be lower than during the peak-to-trough phase, when it would be expected to be higher and rising. In fact, no such regular pattern could be observed.

Another possibility is that it was not the direction of change (i.e., rise or fall) of foreign exchange reserves which guided policy measures, but the *rate* of their change. That is, it may be assumed that whenever the *rate of increase* in reserves accelerated, monetary policy became expansionary; while whenever the rate of increase fell, monetary policy became restrictive. This assumption is examined in Chart 5, part C. By the evidence of this chart, it must be rejected. In fact, for part of the period the opposite is true: from the peak of the 1954–59 cycle (that is, from mid-1956) the rate of increase of reserves goes down during the downward phase and up during the rising phase. That is, when the rate of increase of foreign exchange reserves falls, monetary policy becomes more expansive rather than more restrictive.

Still another possibility which may deserve examination is that the German authorities paid attention not to the actual movement of foreign exchange reserves but to the divergence in the size of reserves from some desired level. This "desired" level could be determined by a probably infinite amount of assumptions, or models. The two simplest assumptions would be: (1) that the "desired" level is that indicated by the trend (which, in turn, can be identified in a variety of ways—a moving average, a linear or log-linear regression, etc.); or (2) that the "desired" size of reserves is a given proportion of imports (or of current transactions). The assumption of a "desired" level of reserves was tested only by the use of the latter variant. This is done in Chart 5, part D. "Desired" reserves were assumed to be a constant proportion of annual imports of goods, equal to the average of 1950–51. Discrepancies between the actual level of reserves and the "desired" level are represented in this chart.

It appears, from Chart 5, part D, that in this sense, i.e., compared with the "desired" level, reserves were increasing throughout most of the period, that is, the ratio of foreign exchange reserves to imports increased continuously. This process went on almost without interruption until 1961. It thus cannot be maintained that monetary policy was designed to preserve a stable ratio of foreign exchange reserves to imports. On the other hand, it may also be seen that until the middle of the trough-to-peak phase of the 1959–62 policy cycle—that is, until

1960—the excess of actual reserves over the "desired" level tended to rise more slowly during the trough-to-peak than in the opposite phases. This would be consistent with an assumption that during the 1950's a given rate of continuous rise in the ratio of foreign exchange reserves was desired and that monetary policy became restrictive when this rate was not achieved, whereas it became expansionary when it was exceeded.

In Chart 5, part E, the target of high employment is examined. The unemployment rate appears, from this chart (as from even a casual look at Chart 4) to be continuously and markedly falling throughout the period. However, no consistent association between this movement and the cycles of monetary measures can be distinguished. It thus does not appear that monetary policy was geared to this target. It may also be mentioned in this connection that the large budgetary surpluses observed during most of the first half of the 1950's were achieved at a time of high unemployment, so that it cannot be assumed either that budgetary policy was employed in pursuance of the target of full or high employment.

In Chart 5, parts F and G, the stable price level target is examined. This is done by using the rates of change in the cost of living and wholesale price indexes, respectively. These rates showed considerable fluctuations only at the beginning of the period, during the Korean crisis and shortly afterwards, while for most of the remaining period the price level appears quite stable. The rates of change in the indexes, in particular of wholesale prices, are quite close to zero and do not fluctuate greatly. What is particularly relevant, however, is the apparent lack of any cyclical regularity. Had monetary policy been intended to maintain price stability, we would expect to find a relatively high rate of price increase during the trough-to-peak phase—that is, when monetary policy becomes restrictive—and the opposite during the peak-to-trough phase. In fact, no such regularity appears at all in the two parts of the chart. Oddly, the cyclical patterns of 1954–59 and 1959–62, especially with regard to the cost of living index, even appear almost as mirror opposites of each other.

The target of a high rate of growth, as measured by the rate of increase of industrial production, is examined in Chart 5, part H. Here some pattern appears, although it is rather weak. It seems that, at the beginning of the trough-to-peak phase, the rate of increase in industrial production rises. However, shortly afterwards it starts falling and this fall continues until about the middle of the peak-to-trough stage, when the rate starts rising. This pattern would certainly be inconsistent with an assumption that monetary policy was intended to maintain a stable rate of increase of production. Monetary policy appears to be restrictive usually when the rate of increase in production falls, whereas the opposite policy would be appropriate for achieving the target under examination. This pattern would be consistent, on the other hand, with an assumption that monetary policy *affected* the growth rate—that restrictive monetary policy led, with a time lag, to a decline of the rate of increase of production, while expansionary monetary policy induced—again with some time lag—a faster rate of increase of production.

3. Summary and Interpretation

From the evidence just analyzed it appears that none of the major targets under examination was, with any consistency, the variable with which monetary policy (and, it should be added, most probably budgetary policy as well) was concerned. The only assumption which did not seem to be refuted was that monetary policy during the 1950's was intended to maintain a steady rate of increase in the ratio of foreign exchange reserves to imports. While such a policy rule is conceivable, the support given to this possibility from the present analysis is probably not strong enough to establish a valid claim for it.

This may lead to one or more of these possible interpretations: (1) The policy instruments under review were manipulated, as a rule, in the service of another target than those examined here; (2) the instruments were used to achieve one of the investigated targets, but this could not be revealed by the present analysis; or (3) policy instruments were indeed used "inconsistently" or, rather, not in adherence to a fixed pattern of rules. They were used on certain occasions for balance-of-payments adjustment, while on others they were used with the object of maintaining price stability or in pursuance of alternative targets.

The first possibility cannot be conclusively rejected. The number of potential target variables is infinite, and it is always possible that one of those which have not been investigated is the real villain of the piece. Likewise, it could always happen that some variant of the targets that have been examined would yield better results. Monetary policy, for instance, might be found to be consistently associated with shifts of foreign exchange reserve levels (or prices, or employment, etc.) away from certain "desired" paths of change in these magnitudes which have not been explored here. Any assertion one way or the other must thus be based only on conjecture and judgment. On these grounds, it would seem highly unlikely that monetary policy was indeed employed consistently in the pursuance of some other untested target. This assertion is supported by the lack of any suggestion of such other policy targets in the literature of German monetary developments. This possibility must, therefore, be dismissed—although no attempt can be made here to offer definitive proof that such a dismissal is warranted.

The two remaining explanations seem to be more probable. A possible deficiency in the method of analysis, it will be recalled, is its failure to distinguish between realized and anticipated values. Thus, if avoiding fluctuations of a certain magnitude is the purpose of policy measures, and these fluctuations are correctly anticipated and successfully averted, the data would not show correlations of policy measures with movements in the target. In the case of Germany, something of this sort may have occurred for price stability. According to frequent and emphatic statements of German policy makers, price stability has been by far the most important target of monetary policy in Germany during the period under review. As will be recalled, the present investigation does not show this. No consistent reaction of monetary policy to changes in the degree of price stability can be detected. This may conceivably be due to the fact that price increases were anticipated accurately, and counteracting policies were taken quickly and decisively enough to prevent these anticipated increases from materializing. The virtually complete stability of prices from 1952 to 1957 might be explained in this way, for instance. It is, of course, very difficult to test such an assumption rigorously, since the process by which policy makers' anticipations were formed is not likely to be easily uncovered. It should be recalled, however, that price fluctuations were not entirely absent. On a number of occasions, price increases were large enough and persistent enough to suggest that further price rises must have been anticipated at those periods; and yet, no restrictive monetary measures are found to have been taken consistently in such periods. A prime example is the period from early 1961 to mid-1962, when monetary policy was expansive despite a relatively high rate of price increase—particularly in the cost of living.

Longer-term observations, on the other hand, lend more credibility to the opinion that price stability was indeed a prime target. In Chart 6, movements of the two price levels (wholesale and cost of living) in Germany are compared with the movements of price levels (arithmetic unweighted averages) in the aggregate of eleven countries: the Group of Ten and Switzerland. It is immediately apparent that prices in Germany tended to rise considerably less than the average—although

CHART 6

Germany: Comparisons of Price Movements

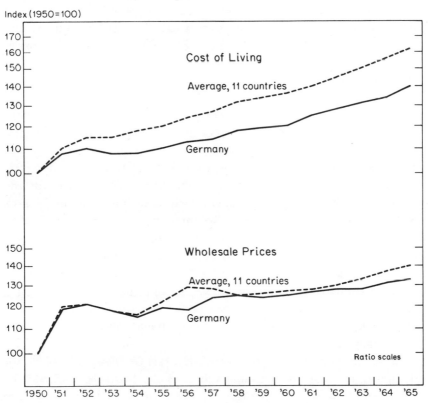

this holds true more for consumer prices than for wholesale prices, and applies more to the first half of the period studied than to the latter half. In the first half of the period, up until around 1957–58, the rate of unemployment in Germany was particularly high (though declining), and the accumulation of foreign exchange reserves persisted throughout these years. Had either full employment or balance-of-payments equilibrium been the overweening target, expansionary monetary and fiscal measures would have been called for; the fact that such measures were not taken suggests that during these years, at least, price stability was a major target in Germany. In other words, it seems probable, by this evidence, that monetary and budgetary policy would have been more expansive throughout the 1950's had not the maintenance of price stability been a prime target for policy makers in Germany. Thus, for instance, the discount rate and other interest rates would have been expected to be generally lower had it not been for this target. At the same time, the former evidence suggests that in formulating changes in short-term monetary and budgetary policy the preservation of stable prices was not invariably, or even in the majority of instances, the guiding rule.

In formulating these short-term reactions it seems most likely, indeed, that no single target consistently dominated the use of monetary policy in Germany. This policy was thus less dogmatic and more flexible than might be inferred from various analyses or statements of policy makers in Germany. On occasion, the policy was aimed at preventing price increases. This is probably true, for instance, for the period 1955–56. On other occasions, such as during parts of 1959 or in late 1960 and in 1961, it must be interpreted as being intended to correct imbalances of payments; while on still other occasions it might have been used to counteract a slump in business conditions.

This analysis was carried somewhat beyond the immediate question of balance-of-payments adjustment. In the light of its mainly negative and inconclusive results, it is time to ask again what *was* the balance-of-payments policy in Germany. The probable answer seems to be, in summary form, as follows.

In the devaluation cycle of September 1949, Germany—although not devaluing the mark to the same extent as the British pound was devalued—established an exchange rate which proved later to have been higher than the rate required for balance-of-payments equilibrium. Thus, for most of the following decade, Germany's balance of payments showed a persistent surplus, and foreign exchange reserves accumulated. There was no attempt to counteract this accumulation owing, presumably, to two considerations. First, starting from a low level of reserves and realizing a fast growth in the amount of trade, the increase in reserves must have been seen by Germany as desirable. Second, a policy to correct imbalances of payments would have called for price increases, while the maintenance of price stability must have been regarded a prime target in view of Germany's earlier inflationary experience. At the same time, temporary downward movements of reserves in the late 1950's were not a cause for major concern in view of the large size of reserves, and thus did not call necessarily for an adjusting policy. This largely "neutral" policy was changed in the early 1960's. At that time, the relatively high level of interest rates in Germany, combined with expectations for revaluation of the mark which were formed by the persistent German surpluses, attracted large amounts of short-term capital from abroad. Monetary policy reacted first in a restrictive way, that is, in a disadjusting direction. At that stage, however, such a policy was self-defeating, since the increased interest rates acted more to increase liquidity by attracting more foreign capital than they contributed to the reduction of liquidity by reducing domestic borrowing. Also, foreign resistance to the persistent large-scale accumulation of reserves in Germany became much more severe than it had been earlier. In late 1960, as a result, monetary policy was changed in the expansive direction required for balance-of-payments adjustment. In March 1961, this was combined with an upward revaluation of the mark by 5 per cent. In the following years, policy reaction to upward disturbances mainly took the form of special measures intended to influence capital movements—that is, to discourage the flow of capital to Germany—such as the tax on income from German bonds held by foreigners, which was announced in 1964. Balance-of-payments adjustment does not appear to have been a major target in these years either: an accumulation of reserves still does not seem to be considered a disturbance, while temporary falls in reserves were not of major concern due to the high level of reserves. The assumption of policy makers in Germany appears to have been that income and price developments independent of Germany's monetary policy, and in particular developments in Germany's major trading partners, would restore equilibrium to Germany's balance of payments before an unduly large decline of reserves took place. Over-all monetary and fiscal policy thus has not been primarily tied to balance-of-payments requirements.

5

THE NETHERLANDS

1. Policy Instruments

MONETARY POLICY

The Netherlands Bank, the central bank in the Netherlands, has gradually changed in character. Some acts affecting the Bank's structure, powers, and functions have been adopted since World War II. The Bank's constitution and the definition of its functions are incorporated primarily in the Act of April 1948.

The Netherlands Bank is almost entirely independent of the government. Its Board of Managers and its President are appointed by the Crown for periods of seven years. Representatives of the government participate in meetings of the larger Bank Council in an advisory capacity. The Finance Minister may formally give instructions to the Board of Managers; the latter is entitled in this case to present its objections to the Crown, which then has to make public both the arguments and counterarguments and the final decisions it reaches. In effect, no such instructions have ever been given since the 1948 Act, and the Bank may thus be regarded as independent of the Ministry of Finance.

Banking institutions in the Netherlands vary widely in functions and structure. The greater part of banking transactions, however, are conducted by regular commercial banks. These are highly concentrated: a few large banks, each with a large number of branches (up to 200–250), play a dominant role. The assets of the four largest banks amount to some 60 per cent of the total assets of commercial banks, and those of the thirty-three "representative" banks to 95 per cent. The high measure of concentration and the ease of communication may be important reasons for the tendency of the Netherlands Bank to act as much as possible by agreement with the banks rather than by directives and coercion; these reasons also contribute to the high level of mutual understanding which is found between the Bank and the commercial banks.

The Netherlands Bank employs primarily the three classical instruments of monetary policy: changes in the discount rate, changes in minimum-reserve ratios of the banks, and open-market operations. To a lesser extent, it also applies quantitative credit controls.

The Discount Rate. Lending by the Netherlands Bank to commercial banks takes three forms. First, it may be done by discounting at the Bank. Eligible for discounting is short-term paper, such as Treasury bills or commercial bills of not over 105 days to maturity. More often, banks will resort to the second alternative, which is receiving advances on current account against the pledge of collateral—usually of Treasury bills. The rate charged by the Bank on these advances is one-half of 1 per cent above the discount rate. Finally, the Bank may buy Treasury paper from the banks with a repurchase stipulation. Technically, the Netherlands Bank regards such a transaction as the equivalent of a lending operation rather than an open-market operation.

In general, lending by the Bank to the commercial banks is very slight, and so are the absolute fluctuations in the amount of lending. Borrowing from the Bank is considered an emergency act, intended for the shortest duration, rather than one intended to add reserves to the borrowing bank for any length of time.

Changes in the discount rate thus have a very slight impact on the size of the banking system's reserves, since the amount of borrowing from the Bank is generally insignificant in relation to the size of reserves. However, the discount rate is considered an important yardstick. Changes in it are supposed to reflect the intentions of the Netherlands Bank, thus giving a directive to the commercial banks with regard to the tightening or relaxation of credit supply. A conventional semiautomatic relationship exists between the discount rate and the commercial banks' interest on their lending. Usually, the rate charged on lending to prime borrowers from the banks is about 2 per cent above the discount rate, although it could not fall below the level of 5 per cent.

Minimum-Reserve Ratios. Minimum-reserve policy was, most often, the major tool of the Netherlands Bank after 1954. Although the

Bank was empowered by law to impose minimum-reserve ratios on the banking system, it preferred to do so by agreement. In February 1954 a gentlemen's agreement was concluded between the Bank and some forty commercial banks which in their aggregate constituted the overwhelming majority of the banking system. According to the agreement, the participating banks were required to maintain balances at the Netherlands Bank at a ratio to their deposits determined by the Bank. Subject to this requirement were all sight and time deposits, excluding saving deposits and deposits in foreign currency. The ratio is the same for all types of banks and deposits covered by the agreement. It was not, however, to exceed 15 per cent, and the Netherlands Bank undertook not to raise it above 10 per cent without first selling Treasury paper in the open market on a large scale. In fact, the ratio has always stayed within the 10 per cent limit. The lower limit of fluctuations in the ratio was 4 per cent for most of the time. During 1963, however, it was reduced to zero and has stayed at that level since; that is, the minimum-reserve ratio has not been used as a policy instrument since mid-1963. Before that, on the other hand, changes in the ratio had been rather frequent.

The gentlemen's agreement was concluded at a time when commercial banks were extremely liquid due to an influx of foreign exchange. Market rates of three-month Treasury bills came down to as low as .4 per cent, and the Netherlands Bank was not equipped to eliminate liquidity to the desired extent by open-market operations. The reason for the highly liquid position of the banks is well reflected in the agreement itself. Given its importance, this part of the agreement deserves to be quoted:

"In view of the desire of the Netherlands Bank that the commercial banks should make a contribution towards financing the greatly increased stock of gold and foreign exchange the undersigned [name of bank] is prepared to enter into a gentlemen's agreement with the Netherlands Bank, directed to the maintenance at the Netherlands Bank of a cash reserve adaptable in relation to the movement in the stock of gold and foreign exchange." [1]

This relationship was explained by the Netherlands Bank in terms of equity:

". . . the central bank must be supplied with . . . resources for the

[1] Preamble to the gentlemen's agreement, *Netherlands Bank Report*, 1953, p. 176.

purpose of holding [stock of gold and foreign exchange]. Unless it is desired that these resources shall be provided by the Treasury, that is to say at the cost of the taxpayer, they will have to come from the banks—which in our modern national economy provide a part of the money in circulation, just as much as the Netherlands Bank does, and enjoy the resulting benefits in the form of interest. It is no more than reasonable that, as against these benefits, the banks should also contribute towards providing the means for carrying the international cover for the country's money." [2]

The exceptions to the rule of behavior indicated in these passages are also explained in terms of equity. Suppose credit supply increases due to some autonomous factor. As a result of this expansion, foreign exchange reserves fall. There would be no need under these circumstances to increase commercial bank profits by increasing their lending capacity, since the banks already had their credit raised at the beginning of the process. For such reasons, the Netherlands Bank stated that the relationship of the reserve ratio to gold and foreign exchange reserves should not be entirely automatic, but that the Bank would investigate the reasons for the movements of foreign exchange reserves in each case.

Open-Market Operations. Until 1952, open-market operations were conducted by the Treasury. In July 1952 an agreement between the Treasury and the Netherlands Bank specified that the former would limit itself to issuing new Treasury paper when old paper falls due, and since that time open-market operations have been conducted by the Netherlands Bank. But this does not rule out other financial operations by the Treasury which, as will be noted later, have the same effect as open-market operations.

Although the Bank is empowered to deal in a variety of papers, its stock—and its operations—have been restricted to Treasury paper. These are mainly Treasury bonds with a maturity of one to five years. The stock of this paper held by the Bank at the beginning of its operations, in 1952, was later replenished by converting part of the Treasury's book debt to the Bank into Treasury paper, as well as by the transfer—against Treasury paper—of claims on the EPU from the Bank to the Treasury.

[2] *Ibid.*, p. 79.

Open-market operations are not transacted with commercial banks. They are handled by special brokers which buy and sell both for their clients and on their own account, financing the latter transactions by borrowing on the call-money market and, on occasion, by resorting to rediscounting at the Netherlands Bank. While the greater part of the Treasury paper which serves as instrument in open-market operations is held by banking institutions, a substantial proportion is also held by others, such as institutional investors, corporations, or households.

Open-market operations appear most of the time to be periodic rather than continuous: they are usually concentrated within short periods and not conducted gradually in small amounts.

Quantitative Controls. The Netherlands Bank is entitled by law to impose quantitative (as well as qualitative) restrictions on credit. In 1954, the Bank also concluded a gentlemen's agreement with the banks to that effect. The provisions of this agreement were not implemented; but on one occasion, between the fall of 1957 and the spring of 1958, the Bank tried to impose credit ceilings by charging penalty rates on the amounts by which the Bank's lending to commercial banks exceeded specified ceilings. In 1960, a new gentlemen's agreement was concluded by which quotas may be imposed on each bank's credit according to a uniform formula relating the size of credit to its size at some base period. A commercial bank which exceeds its quota would have to deposit at the Netherlands Bank, interest-free, an amount equal to the excess. In July 1961, the banks were directed under the stipulations of this agreement not to let the size of their lending exceed that of the base period (which was either the last quarter of 1960 or the corresponding month of the previous year) by more than 15 per cent. After that date, the banks were allowed to increase lending by .5 per cent per month. Since August 1962, it was found that this restriction was not effective; the actual size of credit was below the size permitted. The restrictions were removed altogether in January 1963. In September 1963, however, they were renewed and remained in effect until the end of the period investigated. The average amount of each bank's credit during the first half of 1963 was taken as the base. By end of September 1963, the amount of the banks' lending should not have exceeded the base amount by more than 5 per cent; from that month on, expansions of credit by 1 per cent or .5 per cent per month were allowed, for a total of 3 per cent (of the base amount) during the last quarter of 1963, 9 per cent in 1964, and 10 per cent in 1965.

In the last few years of the period, the Netherlands Bank thus appears to have used quantitative restrictions of credit to a significant extent. The Bank has also, on a few occasions, exercised its authority to restrict certain types of credit.

Occasionally, the Bank tried to prevent what it considered an excessive credit expansion by "moral suasion." Due to the close relationship between the Bank and commercial banks, this may have had some effect. However, in general, the Bank did not rely on this means as an important policy instrument.

FISCAL AND DEBT POLICY

The central government's budget consists of an ordinary and an extraordinary section. The latter always shows a large deficit—its expenditures may be as much as five or six times larger than its revenues. In the ordinary budget, on the other hand, a surplus is normally maintained. Most of the time the surplus in the ordinary budget is smaller than the deficit in the extraordinary budget; that is, total expenditures exceed total revenues. The difference is financed, usually, by borrowing from the public.

The central government maintains a strong influence on local budgets. The major source of the municipalities' normal revenue is transfers from the central government, which assigns 12 per cent of its tax revenues to the Municipalities Fund and, in addition, finances major local expenditures such as the costs of police and education. Borrowing by the municipalities is also largely subject to regulation and control by the central government in the form of general quantitative ceilings, ceilings on the rate of interest, and requirements for ad hoc approval of borrowing by the government.

The Treasury's cash balances are held exclusively at the Netherlands Bank, while those of local authorities are held outside it. According to the 1948 Bank Act, the Treasury is entitled to automatic advances from the Bank within fl. 150 million; beyond that, current advances to the Treasury may be given at the Bank's discretion. In effect, such advances have been negligible, usually nonexistent. The

Bank extends credit to the government, instead, by purchasing Treasury bills. Variations in the size of this credit too are usually not considerable. In the earlier years of the period the Bank held a substantial book claim on the Treasury. From early 1952 this was gradually diminished until it disappeared completely by the beginning of 1958. On the other hand, in the earlier part of the period, the government maintained "special deposits" at the Bank, representing the counterpart funds of foreign aid. These grew considerably until early 1952, but declined continuously from then on until they too disappeared in early 1958.

Thus, until 1958 the movement in the government's net indebtedness to the Netherlands Bank was dominated by the movement of the Treasury's book debt and "special deposits," and to some extent by the movement of Treasury bills. Since then, the major sources of variations in the size of this indebtedness are the Treasury bills and, even more often, government's deposits. The latter are a highly fluctuating category: weekly or monthly changes in them are very large in comparison with longer-term movements.

Besides financing budgetary deficits, the government very often conducts financial transactions with the public for the exclusive purpose of affecting monetary conditions. It may, for instance, borrow from the public and deposit the proceeds at the Netherlands Bank. Changes in the government's net indebtedness to the Bank thus reflect not only the cash balance of its budgetary operations but also its financial transactions with the public. To an extent, therefore, the government conducts financial operations which have the same effect as, and may be regarded as a substitute for, open-market operations of the Bank.

2. *Statistical Analysis*

Movements of foreign exchange reserves in the Netherlands do not present any cyclical pattern. An attempt to divide the whole period into cycles and use cyclical analysis does not, therefore, seem to be very useful. However, though a strong upward trend of reserves is apparent, a substantial number of episodes in which reserves declined, or rose with particular rapidity, makes the analysis of policy reactions to balance-of-payments disturbances possible.

In Table 7, the period is thus divided into subperiods according

TABLE 7

The Netherlands: Movements of Policy Variables During Subperiods of Disturbances

Subperiod	Foreign Exchange Reserves (indication of disturbance) (1)	Discount Rate (2)	Market Rate for 3-Month Treasury Bills (3)	Reserve Ratio Requirements (4)	Open-Market Operations (net) (5)	Netherlands Bank Claims on Commercial Banks (6)
I–IV 1950	rise	− raised	* stable	a	a	n.a.
IV 1950–III 1951	fall	+ raised	− falls	a	a	− rise
III 1951–II 1953	rise	+ lowered	+ falls	a	− sales	− fall
II 1953–II 1954	rise slightly	* stable	+ falls	a	− sales	* stable
II 1954–I 1956	stable	stable	rises	stable	no trend	stable
I 1956–III 1957	fall	+ raised	+ rises	− lowered	* no operations	− rise
III 1957–I 1959	rise	+ lowered	+ falls	− raised	− sales	− fall
I–IV 1959	stable	raised	rises	lowered	purchases	insignificant
IV 1959–IV 1961	rise	* stable	+ falls	− raised	* no trend	insignificant
IV 1961–I 1963	stable	no trend	no trend	lowered	purchases	insignificant
I–IV 1963	rise	* stable	* stable	+ lowered	* no operations	insignificant
IV 1963–II 1964	fall	+ raised	+ rises	a	+ sales	insignificant
II–IV 1964	rise	* stable	n.a.	a	* no operations	insignificant
IV 1964–II 1965	stable	stable	n.a.	a	* no operations	insignificant

(continued)

TABLE 7 (concluded)

Subperiod	Netherlands Bank Net Claims on Government (7)	Netherlands Bank Total Domestic Claims (8)	Commercial Bank Lending to Public (rate of change) (9)	Money Supply (rate of change) (10)	"Primary and Secondary Liquidity" (rate of change) (11)	Budgetary Balance (12)
I–IV 1950	− fall	n.a.	n.a.	n.a.	n.a.	− surplus
IV 1950–III 1951	* no trend	− rise	− rises	+ falls	n.a.	− smaller surplus
III 1951–II 1953	− fall	− fall	− falls	+ rises	n.a.	− larger surplus
II 1953–II 1954	+ rise	+ rise	+ rises	* stable	* stable	+ balanced
II 1954–I 1956	rise	rise	falls	falls	falls	balanced
I 1956–III 1957	− rise	− rise	+ falls	+ falls	+ falls	− deficit
III 1957–I 1959	− fall	− fall	− falls	+ rises	+ rises	* deficit
I–IV 1959	no trend	no trend	rises	falls	falls	surplus
IV 1959–IV 1961	− fall	− fall	− falls	+ rises	+ rises	+ no trend
IV 1961–I 1963	no trend	rise	falls	stable	rises	deficit
I–IV 1963	− fall	− fall	* stable	* stable	− falls	− smaller deficit
IV 1963–II 1964	− rise	− rise	− rises	* stable	* stable	− larger deficit
II–IV 1964	− fall	− fall	− falls	* stable	+ rises	* deficit
IV 1964–II 1965	n.a.	n.a.	n.a.	rises	stable	n.a.

Note: + indicates a movement in the direction required for balance-of-payment adjustment.
   − indicates a movement in the opposite direction.
   * indicates no movement or a very slight one.

n.a. = not available.
a not applicable.

to the fluctuations of the balance of payments. This division is based on the movements of foreign exchange reserves until 1958, and from 1958 onward, on the IMF data of surpluses and deficits in the balance of payments. The latter series almost invariably gives results similar to those provided by the series on foreign exchange reserves.

Starting with the discount rate, it may be seen that this variable is changed most often in the direction that would be required for balance-of-payments adjustment. Only in one subperiod—during 1950—is an opposite movement found; while in a few other episodes in which balance-of-payments adjustment would have required a change in one direction or the other, the discount rate remained stable. To further test this relationship, Table 8 examines the balance-of-payments movements during all quarters in which changes were made in the discount rate. It appears, again, that discount rate changes were overwhelmingly consistent with balance-of-payments requirements. This is true particularly with regard to all the changes made before 1962. Out of fourteen such discount rate movements, only one was in the opposite direction to the requirements of adjustment; three took place when no balance-of-payments adjustment was required; and ten could be explained by the requirements for balance-of-payments adjustment.

To test this association still further, Table 8 also presents a description of the movements of alternative target variables. It appears that the price stability target performs, in general, about as well as the balance-of-payments adjustment target—and better from 1962 on. On the basis of this evidence, one could not assert that the discount rate was used exclusively for balance-of-payments adjustment. It is evident that the requirements of the two targets—balance-of-payments adjustment and price stability—coincided most of the time, so that the discount rate changes were consistent with both. This coincidence of the two targets may be expected in a country whose share in world trade is not very large, while the share of trade in its own economy is substantial. Changes in conditions abroad are likely to have only small impact on the trade of such a country; while inflationary or deflationary pressures within the economy, which are likely to be reflected in price movements, may be expected to have an immediate and substantial effect on the country's trade balance.

Movements of the other two targets represented in Table 8—industrial production and employment—do not reveal any consistent pattern

TABLE 8

The Netherlands: Changes in the Discount Rate and
Movements of Policy Targets

Quarter	Discount Rate (1)	Foreign Exchange Reserves (2)	Price Level (Cost of Living Index) Compared with Trend (3)	Industrial Production (rate of change) (4)	Unemployment (5)
III 1950	raised	* stable	* stable	+ rises	* stable
II 1951	raised	+ fall	+ rises	− falls	* stable
I 1952	lowered	+ rise	− rises	* stable	+ rises
III 1952	lowered	+ rise	+ falls	* stable	+ rises
II 1953	lowered	+ rise	+ falls	− rises	− falls
I 1956	raised	* stable	* stable	* stable	* stable
III 1956	lowered	− fall	* stable	* stable	− falls
IV 1956	raised	+ fall	* stable	* stable	* stable
III 1957	raised	+ fall	+ rises	− falls	− rises
I 1958	lowered	+ rise	+ falls	+ falls	+ rises
II 1958	lowered	+ rise	+ falls	* stable	+ rises
IV 1958	lowered	+ rise	+ falls	− rises	+ stable-high
I 1959	lowered	+ rise	+ falls	* stable	− falls
IV 1959	raised	* stable	+ rises	+ rises	+ falls
II 1962	raised	− rise	+ rises	− falls	* stable
I 1963	lowered	* stable	− rises	+ falls	* stable
I 1964	raised	* stable	+ rises	* stable	* stable
II 1964	raised	* stable	+ rises	+ rises	* stable

Note: + The change in the target variable would justify the direction of change in the discount rate.
− The change in the target variable would justify the opposite direction.
* The change in the target variable would call for no change in the discount rate.

in relation to discount rate changes. It appears from the evidence of this table that these two were not usually regarded as the targets at the service of which the discount rate is employed.

Column 3 in Table 7 shows the changes in another short-term interest rate, which is often quoted in the Netherlands: the rate (yield) of three-month Treasury bills. As may be seen from Chart 7, the

CHART 7

The Netherlands: Time Series of Selected Variables

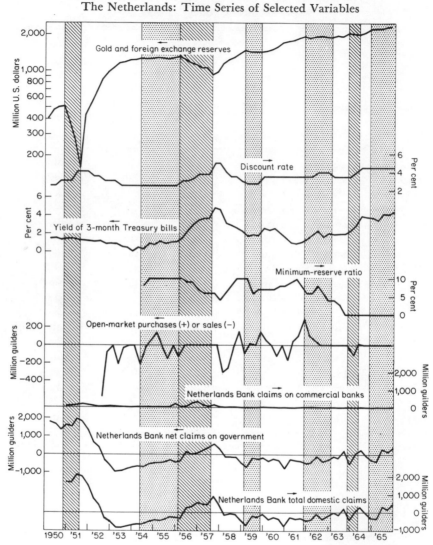

CHART 7 *(concluded)*

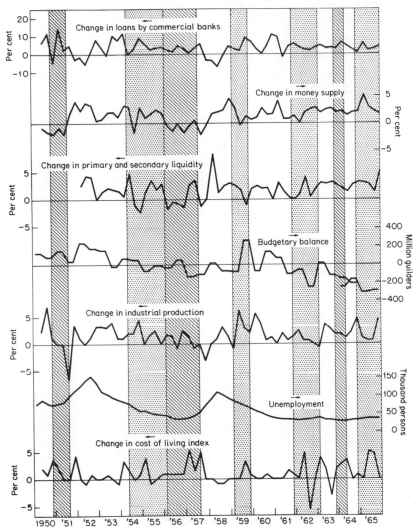

Note: Diagonal-line areas represent periods of downward imbalances; gray areas represent stability; and white areas represent upward imbalances.

movements of this rate and of the discount rate are highly correlated. It is thus not surprising that Table 7 shows this variable also moving in a way which is, by and large, consistent with the requirements for balance-of-payments adjustment.

In column 4 of Table 7, movements of the minimum-reserve ratio are described for the period for which this instrument was used, that is, from 1954 to 1963. It appears that throughout these years, this variable was changed mostly in a direction *opposite* to the requirements of balance-of-payments adjustment. This relationship is examined in greater detail in Table 9, which lists all the quarters in which the reserve ratio was changed.[3] The impression which emerges from this table is very clear: the rule that the minimum-reserve ratio is changed in the opposite direction to balance-of-payments requirements was observed consistently, with only few exceptions. Out of eighteen quarters in which the ratio was changed, this held true in thirteen instances, while the opposite held true only four times. The association is even more striking for the period prior to mid-1961. This relationship might have been expected, of course, from the very justification given to concluding the gentlemen's agreement, which established and governed the instrument under consideration, and the mode of operations which the agreement specified. As will be remembered, the agreement stated that movements of the minimum-reserve ratio should, as a rule, be positively correlated with movements of foreign exchange reserves: when the latter rise, the ratio should be raised, and vice versa. This, of course, is a policy which works in the opposite direction from what balance-of-payments adjustment would require. The agreement did not call for a strict adherence to this rule, and the Netherlands Bank was always careful to point this out. Yet, throughout the 1950's this was virtually an airtight rule.[4] Only in the 1960's

[3] Excluded from this table are the changes through the first half of 1954. When reserve requirements were first introduced, by the gentlemen's agreement of February 1954, the rate was determined at 5 per cent, and was then increased each month by 1 per cent, until it reached the level of 10 per cent. These increases, however, should be regarded as part of the gradual process of establishing a starting ratio of 10 per cent.

[4] Just a single exception is found, in the last quarter of 1957: while foreign exchange reserves were rising, the minimum-reserve ratio was lowered, rather than raised as was the normal practice. This, however, may perhaps be ascribed to a time lag and imperfections of knowledge and measurement. The ratio was lowered in October 1957; foreign exchange reserves were falling until September 1957, and then started rising only just before the ratio was lowered.

apparently regarded as a desirable feature, not strong enough to be considered a disturbance. Monetary policy during these later years appears, thus, to be less concerned with balance-of-payments developments. It is now employed in the service of other targets as well—to a large extent, probably, the target of price stability.[7] It is important to note that the change in pattern came at a period of generally rising—albeit slowly—foreign exchange reserves. An element of asymmetry may be indicated by this; however, it would be necessary to contrast a long period of slightly and gradually declining reserves with this period in order to check this indication, and such cannot be found.

Budgetary policy was oriented in a direction contrary to the requirements of balance-of-payments adjustment more often than it was in the direction which adjustment would require. This may be consistent with the hypothesis that automatic income effects of the trade balance were considered more than sufficient to achieve the necessary adjustment, so that some counteraction was called for. In view of the generally small size of either budgetary surpluses or deficits, however, a conclusion that budgetary policy was indeed fashioned in this way may not be justified. It seems that this policy was usually intended to be "neutral," not only in relation to balance-of-payments developments, but also with regard to other major targets. It would be even less correct to conclude that the combined pattern of monetary-fiscal policy adhered to the well-known policy mix, assigning monetary policy to the pursuance of balance-of-payments equilibrium and fiscal policy for "domestic" targets. Only one episode—1956–57—might be explained in this way. In this case, restrictive monetary policy could have been intended to adjust the balance of payments and expansionary fiscal policy, to counteract unemployment and slack production. In the two other episodes of significant budgetary deficits, increases in the discount rate are again found; but on these occasions the opposite movements could not be explained by the requirements of balance-

---

[7] This impression is supported by the observation of quantitative credit restrictions. Their introduction in 1961 came at a time of rising foreign exchange reserves; their relaxation during 1962–63, at a time of stable reserves; and their reintroduction, in 1963, again at a period of accumulating reserves. This would be consistent with the pattern of the 1950's, of a counteracting policy. Yet the quantitative restrictions since 1963 do not seem to be affected by the balance-of-payments position. On the other hand, these years are characterized by substantial price rises, which could explain the introduction and preservation of credit restrictions.

of-payments equilibrium, on the one hand, and domestic targets on the other.

The rate-of-exchange instrument was used on only one occasion, March 1961, when the rate was lowered (and the currency appreciated) by 5 per cent. During the preceding period, foreign exchange reserves were rising, and the economy was showing inflationary tendencies. This, indeed, is a combination in which currency appreciation would be a proper measure. However, the development of reserves and prices prior to the revaluation does not seem to be radically different in size or other circumstances than it was on many other occasions. The use of currency revaluation in this instance may thus presumably be explained, as, indeed, was insistently argued by policy makers when the measure was taken, only by the fact of the similar German measure. Since Germany is a major trading partner of the Netherlands, the appreciation of the mark could be expected to strongly intensify the trends of rising foreign exchange reserves and rising prices in the Netherlands. Speculation could have contributed to it even further. It was thus not so much actual developments as the anticipations of strongly intensified trends which led to the Dutch measure. The fact that a change in the exchange rate could be represented as following the lead of another country must have also been a strong contributing factor. An additional explanation could be the realization that a long-term accumulation of foreign exchange reserves may be an indication of fundamental disequilibrium. Despite this episode, it is obvious that during the period surveyed changing the exchange rate was not considered a proper instrument for balance-of-payments adjustment in the Netherlands.

TABLE 9

The Netherlands: Changes in the Minimum-Reserve Ratio
and Movements of Policy Targets

Quarter	Minimum-Reserve Ratio (1)	Foreign Exchange Reserves (2)	Price Level (Cost of Living Index) Compared with Trend (3)	Industrial Production (rate of change) (4)	Unemployment (5)
II 1956	lowered	− fall	* stable	* stable	− falls
IV 1956	lowered	− fall	* stable	* stable	* stable
I 1957	lowered	− fall	− rises	* stable	* stable
IV 1957	lowered	+ rise	− rises	+ falls	+ rises
I 1958	raised	− rise	− falls	− falls	− rises
II 1958	raised	− rise	− falls	− falls	− rises
III 1958	raised	− rise	− falls	+ rises	− rises
II 1959	lowered	− fall	+ falls	− rises	+ falls-high
III 1960	raised	− rise	− falls	+ rises	+ falls
I 1961	raised	− rise	− falls	* stable	+ falls
II 1961	raised	− rise	− falls	* stable	* stable
III 1961	lowered	+ rise	* stable	* stable	* stable
IV 1961	lowered	+ rise	− rises	* stable	* stable
II 1962	raised	− rise	+ rises	* stable	* stable
III 1962	lowered	* stable	+ falls	* stable	* stable
IV 1962	lowered	− fall	+ falls	+ falls	* stable
II 1963	lowered	+ rise	− rises	* stable	* stable
III 1963	lowered	− fall	+ falls	− rises	* stable

Note: See Table 8 for explanation of symbols used. Here minimum-reserve ratio replaces discount rate.

did this practice change, and exceptions to it became as frequent as observance of it.

The competing targets are also observed in Table 9. It appears that the minimum-reserve ratio was definitely not used to maintain price stability; the ratio was changed in the opposite direction, as a rule, to that which price stability would require—a relationship which must be attributed to the correlation between price movements and balance-of-payments disturbances noted earlier. Once more, this seems to change during the 1960's. From 1962 on (to the effective abolishment of the use of this instrument towards the end of 1963), changes in the reserve ratio were mostly consistent with the requirements of price stability, and might be explained by this target. On the other hand, no consistent relationship appears between changes in the minimum-reserve ratio, on the one hand and either the level of unemployment or the level of industrial production, on the other. It appears quite safe to conclude that, like the discount rate, the minimum-reserve ratio instrument was not generally employed either to serve the ends of high industrial production or high employment.

The third monetary instrument, open-market operations, is represented in column 5 of Table 7. It appears to move less often in the direction required for balance-of-payments adjustment than it does in the opposite direction; but over all, the relation between this instrument and the movements of foreign exchange reserves seems to be much weaker than it appears to be in the use of either the discount rate or the minimum reserve ratio. Open-market operations were taken, we recall, rather sporadically. They seemed to have been intended most of the time to "stabilize the market"—that is, to help maintain an existing level of interest rates. Apparently, they were considered a secondary tool rather than a major one and were not universally employed in pursuit of one of the major global targets.

Commercial bank borrowing from the Netherlands Bank is described in column 6 of Table 7. It will be recalled that as a rule, the amount of this borrowing was very small, hence changes in it were of no quantitative significance either. In only two episodes did the amount of borrowing rise to considerable proportions. In the two instances of substantial declines of foreign exchange reserves which may be distinguished, during 1951 and 1956–67, this item increased materially; in both instances it dropped back to its normal low level in the subsequent periods of rising foreign exchange reserves. These, of course, are movements in an opposite direction to the requirements of balance-of-payments adjustment. It should also be noted that they are in a direction opposite to that which movements of the discount rate should engender: that is, in both episodes, commercial bank borrowing increased when the discount rate was raised and decreased when the discount rate was lowered.

The net indebtedness of the government to the Netherlands Bank (excluding changes due to open-market operations) is represented next, in column 7 of Table 7. It appears immediately that its movements were usually in a direction opposite to the requirements of balance-of-payments adjustment: the indebtedness rises, most often, when foreign exchange reserves fall, and falls when reserves rise. A glance at column 12, which describes the budgetary balance, will show that this pattern is quite similar to that of the movements of the budgetary balance, but it is even more consistent in its negative relationship to the balance of payments. The greater consistency must be attributed, thus, to the government's financial transactions with the public—in distinction to the "real" transactions which find expression in the budget. In other words, the government must have conducted its equivalent of open-market operations—borrowing from the public and depositing at the central bank, or repaying (lending to) the public by drawing on deposits at the Bank—in a direction opposite to balance-of-payments requirements. To some extent, this direction seems to have been due to public initiative. When foreign exchange reserves fall and reduce the economy's liquidity, banks (and other potential buyers) are less likely to increase their lending to the government (i.e., to buy Treasury bills or bonds), and more likely to reduce the amount of these assets held by them; and the opposite is true when the economy's liquidity increases by an accumulation of foreign exchange reserves.

Total domestic claims of the Netherlands Bank, the combination of the last three elements (Bank lending to the commercial banks, Bank acquisition of government paper in the open market, and other net lending of the Bank to the government), is represented in column 8 of Table 7. The net claim on the government was usually the main component of this category and accounted for most of the changes in it. Since it (as well as Bank lending to the banks) moved opposite to the requirements of balance-of-payments adjustment, it is of course not surprising to find that so did the combined category. Indeed, this pattern was even more consistent for the total than for each of its components: only a single exception—the period from mid-1953 to mid-1954—appears to violate this inverse relationship. Thus, by the Nurkse-Bloomfield criterion, the Netherlands Bank appears to have played very consistently against the "rules of the game."

Lending by commercial banks to their customers, described in column 9 of Table 7, appears to move in the disadjusting direction. It rises faster than usual when foreign exchange reserves fall, and falls (or rises only much less than the trend) when reserves rise. This inverse relationship seems to be indicated clearly, although there are a few exceptions to it.

Quite the opposite pattern applies to changes in money supply, as is shown in column 10 of Table 7. It moves almost invariably in the direction which balance-of-payments adjustment would require. Money supply and foreign exchange reserves appear clearly to rise together and fall together. Essentially this is true also with regard to another measure of the economy's liquidity, to which much attention is given in the monetary analysis of the Netherlands Bank: the magnitude of "primary and secondary liquidity," [5] which is represented in column 11 of Table 7. Like money supply, which is itself, of course, a major component (roughly two-thirds) of "primary and secondary liquidity," it moves most of the time in the direction indicated by the need for balance-of-payments adjustment, that is, in the same direction as foreign exchange reserves.

Budgetary policy is described in column 12 of Table 7. As has been mentioned before, it appears to run most often in a direction contrary to the requirements of balance-of-payments adjustment. When foreign exchange reserves rise, the government's excess demand falls (that is, its deficit turns to surplus or becomes smaller in absolute magnitude, or a surplus gets bigger); and when reserves fall, the government's excess demand rises. This pattern has its exceptions, but they are few.

To further test the budgetary policy, Table 10 analyzes the episodes in which the budget was clearly either in a surplus or in a deficit position. Movements of foreign exchange reserves are represented in column 2 of the table. It appears, as before, that the budgetary balance behaved most of the time—but not consistently—contrary to what balance-of-payments adjustment would require. The price stability target does not fare better (Table 10, column 5). The industrial production and employment targets, shown in columns 3 and 4, respectively, also do not appear to be generally served by

---

[5] The "primary" liquidity is money supply, defined in the conventional way. "Secondary" liquidity includes: (1) claims on the government; (2) claims on the local authorities; and (3) claims on money-creating institutions, i.e., time deposits and day-to-day loans, foreign-currency balances of residents, and balances in savings accounts.

price stability, on the one hand, and employment and output on the other. In this year changes in circumstances abroad were, apparently, particularly important and must have played a significant part in the Netherlands' balance-of-payments situation. While most often, as has been pointed out before, balance-of-payments deficits were accompanied by domestic expansions, this episode was an exception. Foreign-exchange reserves were falling and prices were rising rapidly, while unemployment was rising and industrial production falling. The budgetary policy during those years appears to be expansive, as would be required by the targets of employment and production. Monetary policy, on the other hand, if judged by the movements of money supply and interest rates, was restrictive—as would be required by the balance-of-payments equilibrium and price stability targets.

3. Summary and Interpretation

From the preceding analysis it seems clear that, at least during the 1950's, monetary policy was strongly associated with the balance of payments—although in a somewhat intricate manner which, on the surface, appears to involve contradictory tendencies.

A point of major importance is the extremely high share of foreign trade in the economy of the Netherlands. Foreign trade in proportion to national income is higher in the Netherlands than anywhere in Europe (save Luxembourg, which for economic purposes may in effect be considered a region of Belgium). Any change of a given proportion in exports or imports carries thus a heavier weight in the Dutch economy than in most other countries. Since the ratio of foreign exchange reserves to trade is not particularly low in the Netherlands, the large trade means also a large size of reserves in relation to income or to money supply. A given proportional change in reserves thus has a particularly large monetary impact there.

Any imbalance of payments has thus a very large automatic impact on the economy of the Netherlands in comparison with other countries; and this inflationary or deflationary impact seems to have been judged too large by the Netherlands policy makers—that is, the impact, by itself, gives too much weight to balance-of-payments adjustment and too little to other targets. Therefore, policy has been directed at counteracting this automatic impact. Thus, the discretionary mone-

TABLE 10

The Netherlands: The Budgetary Balance
and Movements of Policy Targets

Period	Budgetary Balance (1)	Foreign Exchange Reserves (2)	Price Level (Cost of Living Index) Compared with Trend (3)	Industrial Production (rate of change) (4)	Unemploy- ment (5)
I 1950–II 1953	surplus	− rise	* stable	* stable	− rises
IV 1956–IV 1957	deficit	− fall	− rises	+ falls	+ rises
II 1960–II 1961	surplus	− rise	− falls	* stable	+ falls
II 1961–IV 1962	deficit	* rise slightly	* stable	* stable	* stable
II 1963–IV 1964	deficit	+ rise	* stable	− rises	* stable

Note: See Table 8 for explanation of symbols used. Here budgetary balance replaces discount rate.

budgetary policy, which seems to be "neutral" to these targets. In general, budgetary imbalances (surpluses or deficits) were rather small and
apparently played only a minor role in pursuit of short-term targets. During one episode only, from the beginning of the period surveyed to the middle of 1953, were budgetary surpluses large and consistent. As can be seen from Table 10, none of the targets represented
there could explain the surpluses during the period of the early 1950's.
Foreign-exchange reserves were rising rapidly. Price increases were normal, that is, not exceeding their long-term trend, or even slightly below it. Industrial production was also rising at its normal rate, while
employment was even falling. The large surpluses must be explained
either by other targets or as an accidental phenomenon. One explanation sometimes suggested is that budgetary policy was aimed at encouraging long-term growth by accumulating capital through government saving. Another possibility is that the surpluses resulted, as in
Germany, from the planning of military expenditures which did not
in fact materialize.

Another interesting episode of budgetary imbalances is that of 1957.
During that year, there was an obvious contradiction between the requirements of the targets of balance-of-payments equilibrium and

INDEX